**The Internet made easy
by the world's No.1**

AOL.

Email and *More!*

GW00492895

The Internet made easy
by the world's No.1

AOL

Email and More!

Keep in touch with friends and family - instantly

By Nigel Whitfield

CAPSTONE

First published 2002 by
Capstone Publishing Limited (a Wiley company)
8 Newtec Place
Magdalen Road
Oxford OX4 1RE
United Kingdom
http://www.capstoneideas.com

CIP catalogue records for this book are available from the British Library and the US Library of Congress

ISBN 1-84112-188-6

Typeset in 9.5/14pt Fruitiger by
Sparks Computer Solutions Ltd, Oxford, UK
http://www.sparks.co.uk
Printed and bound by
T.J. International Ltd, Padstow, Cornwall

This book is printed on acid-free paper

Contents

C H A P T E R

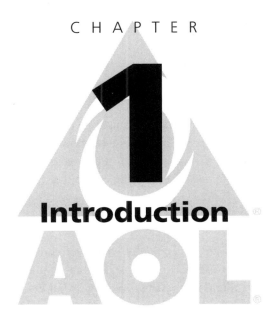

Introduction

To many people, going online is a way to access vast amounts of information from the fabled "super highway." The Net is like a giant library, full of encyclopaedias for looking things up, music to listen to, files to download, and other reference materials.

But there's a lot more to it than that. The online world is a great resource for finding things out, but it's also a community, and a tool for communicating. The snazzy Web pages with movie clips may be popular, but they're dwarfed by the number of email messages sent every day, just to take one example. If the Net really is a library, it's one where there's a lot more talking going on than usual – and as long as you don't break the common sense rules (see **Chapter 10, Online Guidelines**), no one's going to tell you to be quiet.

10 Common sense

Connect your computer to the phone line and it's not just a passive experience – you can take part, communicating with friends, family and other people.

You can find new friends, or keep in touch with distant relatives, without the delays of air mail or the expense of international phone calls.

You might have thought the invention of the phone changed things, but your computer can do much, much more. You can send a photograph of your new baby across the world in minutes, for example. Or hunt through online phone books to catch up with those colleagues who moved to California. Perhaps you'd like to send your partner a quick message while they're at work to remind them to bring home some shopping, without disturbing them. Or you may want to share a problem with other people who've been through the same.

You can do all of this with your computer – and if you connect with AOL, you'll find that you can do it all simply, quickly and cheaply, without having to learn how to use lots of different programs. And that's what this book is all about.

Online with AOL

AOL isn't just a way of connecting to the Internet – it provides you with access to a wealth of services and communities made up from over 33 million people around the world. There are other ways to go online, but AOL is the largest, and you can access it from anywhere in the world.

Not only that, but AOL uses a simple, friendly interface that makes it easy to keep in touch, and also has filtering software to help restrict what your children can do when they go online, so you can let them use the computer with complete confidence.

But what exactly can AOL do to help you communicate? There are plenty of different ways you can keep in touch, and later on in the book you'll find a chapter dedicated to each of them, as well as plenty of tips to help you get to grips with things as quickly as possible.

Email
Email is probably one of the most useful things ever invented – including sliced bread! With email, all you have to do is type a message into your computer,

just like using a word processor, then add the address of the person you want to send it to, click a button with the mouse, and it's gone.

Email is usually delivered in minutes, and sometimes even within seconds, and once you're online, there are no extra charges for sending a message. You can even include pictures or other files with your message, and send them round the world.

So instead of waiting days and paying pounds to post a lengthy document to a colleague, use email – it'll be cheaper and much, much faster.

You can use email to reach lots of people at the same time too, just by adding their addresses to the message, so it's ideal for things like party invites, or keeping in touch with all the different parts of your family in one easy step.

AOL Instant Messenger™

Email may be quick, but you can communicate even faster! The AOL Instant Messenger™ service is just that – you simply type a short note into your computer, click **Send**, and if your friend is online, it'll pop up on their screen for them to read or reply to.

If you don't want to send an email, or you need a quick answer, Instant Message can be ideal. You'll know within seconds whether there's an answer to your question, whether it's "can you buy some milk on the way home from work?" or "where are the new purchase order forms?"

There's no need to check your mail again and again to be sure that the message has got through; an Instant Message lets you know. And with the Buddy List™ feature, you can see whether or not the people you want to reach are online too, so you can quickly say "Good morning" to your mates, or chat about something that's just been announced on the news.

Chat rooms

Instant Message is a great way to chat with one other person, but sometimes you want to do more that that, and that's where chat rooms come in. A chat room is more or less exactly what the name suggests – it's like a room in which people are talking with each other, sometimes just about one thing, sometimes about lots of different things, with conversations going on all at the same time. But of course, instead of using your voice, you type your comments on the keyboard, and read the things that other people say on the screen.

Chat rooms can be frivolous, with people just talking about nothing in particular, or telling jokes. Or they can be deeply technical, with users swapping hints and tips about how to get the best out of a Mark 2 Ford Escort, for example. And you can even find them supportive, letting you tell other people about what a bad day you've had at work, and hearing how their bosses are just as bad, for example.

So whether it's the answer to a particularly thorny problem with homework, a chance to let off steam about the budget, or simply a chat about the weather, a chat room gives you the chance to talk via your keyboard with people all over the world.

Message boards

If a chat room is a little like a public version of the AOL Instant Messenger service, message boards have a similar relationship to email.

Just like email, message boards are a way that you can write something that other people will read later. The difference is that while an email has to be addressed to someone, a message board is like an electronic equivalent of "to whom it may concern," or the notice board outside the village hall.

Message boards are usually dedicated to a specific topic, like films, current affairs, or even lonely hearts. You can choose where to post your message, and then anyone else who is interested in the same topic will see it next time they visit – and they can usually reply too, by posting another message.

That way, you can end up with a discussion, even if all the people taking part are in different time zones. Or you might get the answer to a problem, the perfect recipe for summer pudding, or the address of the best restaurant in your holiday resort.

Groups

Email, message boards, Instant Message, and chat rooms are the building blocks of communicating via AOL; as you can see from the examples we've already given, together they'll cover just about all the different ways you can think of to communicate with other people.

You'll be able to answer questions, meet new friends, keep in touch with colleagues, or do just about whatever you want.

There's one other feature that AOL provides to make it even easier to keep in touch. While there may be millions of people online, the truth is that you'll probably be keeping in touch with a handful, or perhaps several handfuls.

You might have a group of people you exchange messages with for work, and another for your local sports club, and then another set for the family. Some of them might even be in more than one.

AOL's Groups facility lets you collect together other members into a group which can have its own name, and a set of Web pages where people will be able to read about each other, share pictures, or even arrange dates using a shared calendar and one email address for the whole group. And the group is private – only people you've invited to join will be able to see what's on the pages. So if you set up a group for your colleagues, for instance, your boss won't know what you're saying about him, unless you want him to.

Imagine being able to put the dates of your meetings in an easy to use appointment book for everyone to see, with pictures of the venue, or a report of the last party for the friends who couldn't make it.

Groups@AOL brings together all the other ways of communicating so that you can make your own communities from the millions of people online.

What you should know

This book isn't a complete guide to AOL and the Internet – there are far more things that AOL can do than we could hope to fit in here. But whether you're an old hand or you've never used AOL before, it should show you how to keep in touch with old friends and make new ones.

> AAA

In this book, we've referred to many of the parts of AOL by their s, which are special short cuts you can use to reach almost any part of the service. You'll spot s in the text because they are in a different typeface, for example where you see: Visit : **AAA** for more information, you can just type **AAA** into the box at the top of the AOL screen where it says "Enter keywords or Web addresses here."

There are also some keyboard short cuts that you can use – we'll mention some special ones in the appropriate place, but remember that when you look at the menus in AOL, you'll see the keystrokes listed. On a PC running Windows, the keystrokes are done by holding down the Ctrl key and pressing the appropriate letter.

If you're a Mac user, just use the Apple key (which may be labelled Command on some keyboards) instead of Ctrl.

A quick way to go to an , for example, is to press Ctrl-K on a PC or Apple-K on a Mac, which will bring up a box where you can type in an .

Other useful shortcuts are Ctrl-G to get someone's profile and Ctrl-I to send an Instant Message. We'll list others as and when you might need them, but remember that you can always see them just by browsing through the menus.

What's next?

Whatever you want to go online for, the most important part of the experience is the people you'll meet and share information, gossip, or stories with. Whether you want to tiptoe quietly around the virtual libraries of the Internet, catch up on film news, find people you can play games with online, or practise your French by emailing a real Frenchman, communication is the key.

So, turn to the next chapter, and we'll see how you can start to use AOL to keep in touch with your friends and family. If you're already familiar with how to use AOL, you can go straight to the other chapters to find out more about some of the different tools that will help you keep in touch.

If you're not an AOL member already, you can find out how to sign up by visiting the Web page at www.aol.co.uk. You can even use some of the services, like Instant Message and Groups, without having to be a subscriber – there are more details in **Chapter 9, AOL Anywhere**.

9 AIM

CHAPTER

2

Family and Friends

One of the most useful things that you can do when you go online is keep in touch with your family and friends.

The days when people would grow up, go to school, work, marry, and live most of their lives in one area are long since gone. You might work hundreds or even thousands of miles away from where you grew up, and friends that you knew at college or in your last job might move to the other side of the world to follow their career or their heart.

But none of that means that you have to lose touch with them. Just as the jumbo jet and high speed trains have made it easier than ever to move around, so the Internet and other online services have brought people closer together. So your favourite aunt is in Australia? The cost of calling needn't matter, when you can send her an email or chat online for nothing.

In this chapter, we're going to look at some of the ways that AOL can be used to keep in touch with people, and even to help you track down those that you might have lost touch with, or meet new friends.

Although we'll talk about using tools such as email, chat rooms, and the AOL Instant Messenger™ feature, you'll find more details about exactly how to use them further on in the book – we hope that this chapter helps you realise how useful they can be.

As you start to meet people on AOL, one of the things that might surprise you is how open people can be. It's an old stereotype that British people don't tell you much about their emotions, or that they keep themselves to themselves, but going online is like living in a street where everyone knows each other, and talks about absolutely everything!

Why does this happen? Sometimes people will tell you lots of things because they know you're a long way away – it might be much easier to share an embarrassing problem with someone you'll never bump into in the street. And sometimes people just feel able to type things on their keyboard that they would find it very hard to say face to face – after all, no one can see you blush.

Other people simply find that they just click – when you talk online you don't necessarily have to bother with all the usual introductions and things like that. If you've found someone who has a similar interest to you, why not send a quick message saying something like "Hi there. I'm interested in amateur theatre too; we're doing *Salad Days* this summer. How about you?"

Communicating electronically has changed the way many people talk and relate to each other; it's easy, informal, and there are really no set rules (though there are some guidelines in **Chapter 10, Online Guidelines** that you should follow).

10 Common sense

Still not convinced? Here's a quick glimpse of how useful communicating online can be.

A Christmas tale

Imagine it's the Christmas holiday. I've just got home from work, and there are a few things I need to finish off before I can relax.

Signing on to AOL, I can see in my Buddy List window that one of my colleagues is still in the office, so I can send her a quick Instant Message with a reminder that we still have to finish the new book proposal before everyone finishes for their holiday.

Within a couple of minutes, she replies to me, and says that there's a small problem – she can't manage to make the printer on her computer work.

No problem! I know what sort of printer it is, so I pop into one of AOL's chat rooms, where I know there'll be plenty of technical people. I ask if anyone knows where to get new drivers for the printer and someone tells me that they can be downloaded from a Web site.

Another quick Instant Message, and my colleague in the office knows what to download, and I've given her instructions on what to do when she's downloaded the file. Best of all, she doesn't have to worry about whether or not she types the Web page address right – I've included it in the Instant Message, so she just has to click on it, and the file will start downloading.

Meanwhile, I can check my email, and I find an invitation to a Christmas party that's being held at the AOL office. I just need to confirm that I can go, by clicking **Reply** and sending a quick "Yes." And I notice that, especially for people who haven't been there before, the invitation has a Web link in it. Clicking it makes a new window appear on my screen, showing a map from the tube station to the office.

There's another email too, from my sister in America, which she's sent to all the people who are members of our family, via AOL's Groups facility. If I reply, everyone in the family will see the message, so it's a great way to keep them all up to speed, without having to remember the different addresses they all use.

This message, though, doesn't need an answer – it's just to let me know that Susan's added more pictures of her son to the Group Web page. So all I have to do is open the link I've added to my AOL Favourites, and I'm at the Group page.

In the photos section at the bottom, Susan's uploaded all the new pictures, so I can browse through them at my leisure, and even make a copy on my own computer of the ones that I like. It's so much easier than when she used to send me the whole lot every time, and I had to wait ages for them to download.

The Group page also reminds me that there's something else I can do – the calendar section shows it'll soon be the birthday of one of my cousins, so I could quickly visit the AOL Shopping channel and order them a CD. Except that I don't know quite what sort of thing would be appropriate.

Never mind; all I need to do is pop into one of AOL's message boards – perhaps the music one would be a good place to start. I can post a question asking what's the best sort of CD to get for a teenager that won't make me look really old and out of touch. Next time I sign on, I can check the message board again and see what other AOL members have recommended, before ordering the CD.

Now, before I sign off, I just need to sort out a couple of other things. The car needs some urgent attention before I drive off to the country for Christmas, but my usual garage is busy.

Never mind – the AOL message boards can come in handy again – I can post a message asking if anyone can recommend a good place to have a Citroën serviced. And just on a hunch, I'll try something else too.

AOL's Member Directory lets you search for people based on their location, hobbies, and other information. I'll just search for people in the UK, and add the words **classic car** to the search, to see if I can find people with similar interests. I can read the profiles of all the people that the search lists, and then send them an email, asking if they have any recommendations for good mechanics.

And finally, back to my email, where there's a reply from someone who's read the personal ad I left on AOL, wondering if I'd like to meet up for a drink. Could be fun – and maybe I'll find someone to spend Christmas with.

Finding people with AOL

As you can see from the scenario, there's a lot that you can do with AOL. You might not do all those things in one session, but it's perfectly possible. And it can make a tremendous difference in all areas of your life – not just work, or keeping in touch with the family.

The other chapters in this book will show you how to communicate with people using the different tools that AOL provides, but of course you need to know people's addresses before you can contact them electronically.

If you know that someone is online and you're in touch with them another way, the answer is simple – you just ask them for their email address. But you might be trying to find a former colleague, or someone you were at university with, or perhaps a lost family member. Maybe you just want to find people to chat with about a particular interest, or you're looking for love.

Whatever the reason, there are plenty of tools that you can use on AOL and the Internet to try and get in touch with people – and we're going to explain some of them here, so that when you look at the other chapters, you'll already know plenty of people who you can chat to and exchange messages with.

Profiles

One of the key ways of finding people on AOL, or making sure that other people can find you, is Member Profiles. A Profile is simply a short bit of information that you can fill in, which is stored on the AOL computers.

When someone sees you in a chat room, or receives an Instant Message from you, they can click a button to read your Profile. Or they could search through all the profiles for particular words, or locations, to find people that it might be interesting to talk with.

Some people simply won't respond to messages from you if you don't have a profile – they think it's a bit like an introduction at a party. And it's certainly a good idea if your Screen Name doesn't match your real name – after all, it's much easier to chat to someone when you know they're called Nigel and not just "AOLBookWriter" isn't it?

Although it's a good idea to make a Profile, you should remember that they can be searched by all other AOL members, so don't include information that is private. And if you make a Profile for a child, don't give enough information to allow people to identify them, or find out where they live and go to school.

Some people use Profiles to collect email addresses for junk mail, so if you don't want to receive any, it might be a good idea to create an extra Screen Name just for chatting, set to block email, and have no Profile for your main name. You can read about Screen Names and Parental Controls in **Chapter 10, Online Guidelines**

10 It's all in the name

My Profile

Creating a Profile is very easy. All you have to do is go to AOL Keyword: **My Profile** and fill in the form that appears on your screen.

Fill in as much or as little of the form as you like. You could, for example, just give your first name, though many people will find it more useful to add a little more.

You'll see that there are particular boxes for different types of information, but you don't have to stick to the headings. Look at some of the Profiles on

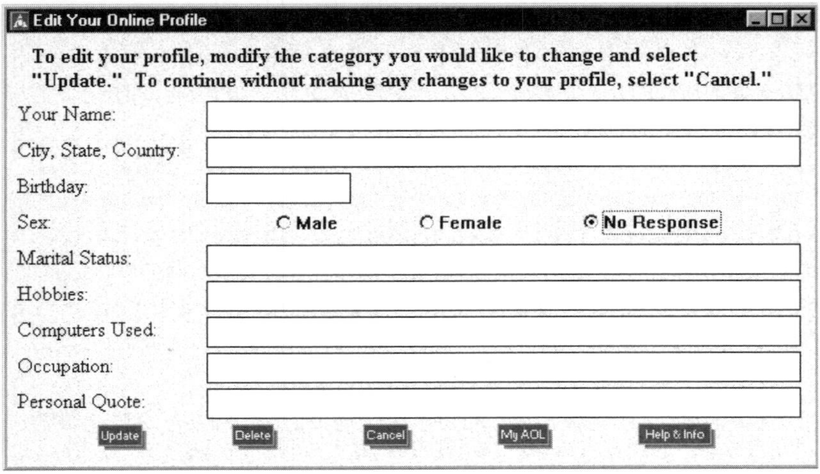

Fig. 2.1 The Edit My Profile screen.

AOL, and you'll see that people have written a mini-essay, spanning all the boxes on the form.

When you're happy with what you've written, click **Update**, and your details will be saved so that other AOL members can look at them.

If you'd like to see what your profile will look like to other people, click **Get Member Profile** on the **People** menu, then type your own Screen Name into the box that appears.

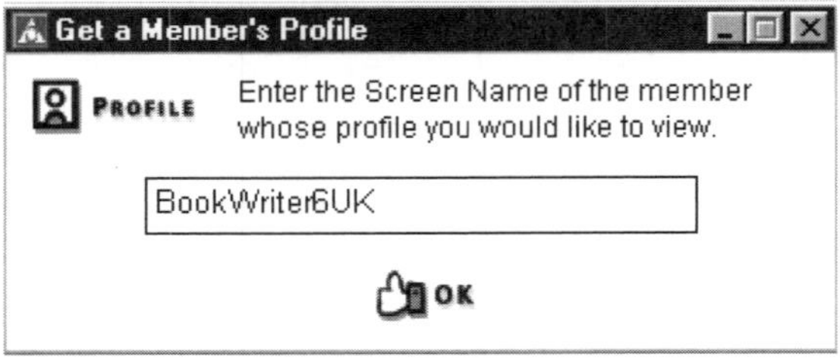

Fig. 2.2 Getting another member's Profile.

Click **OK**, or press the **Enter** key on your keyboard, and in a moment the Profile will appear, looking something like Fig. 2.3.

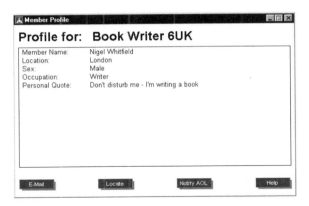

Fig. 2.3 Viewing a Member Profile.

Searching Profiles

So, that's how you create a Profile, but how do you find people with similar interests to yourself? Easy. Go to AOL's **People** menu again, and click **Search People Directory**. The Quick Search screen will appear, looking like this:

Fig. 2.4 The Quick Search screen.

The Quick Search screen is the best way to find many people. Just type in words that you'd like to find in someone's Profile, like "car" or "author." If you'd like to restrict the search to people called Nigel, enter that in the Member Name box, or choose a location, like London, in the Location box. You can also restrict your search to a particular country, if you like, or to people who speak a particular language.

Click **Search** when you're done, and you'll see a list of matching members appear on the screen.

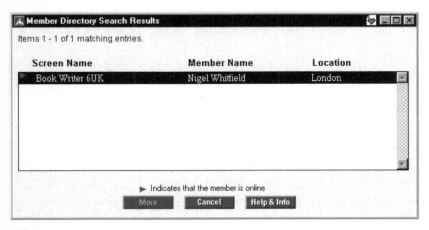

Fig. 2.5   Search Results screen.

To read the Profile for any of the people listed, just double-click on their name, and it will appear, just as your own one did earlier. If you see a red triangle next to one of the names in the list, it means that member is connected to AOL right now, so if you like the look of their Profile, you could try to send them an Instant Message right away.

If **More** at the bottom of the list is showing, then you can click it to get another 20 matches, up to a total of 100.

What about that Advanced search? Well, if you click the **Advanced** tab on the search screen, you'll see the screen in Fig. 2.6.

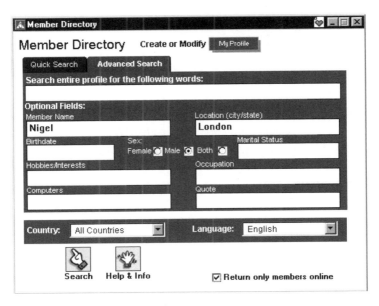

Fig. 2.6   The Advanced Member Search screen.

As you can see, you can enter information in boxes, just like you did when you filled in your own Profile. Of course, if someone's disregarded the names of the boxes when they made their Profile, then this screen won't work quite as well as it should.

> *If you want to have a Profile that people could search to track you down with the Advanced search, as well as a more general one, create another Screen Name that people can use to find you easily. You can learn about creating more names in* **Chapter 10, Online Guidelines***.*

10 It's all in the name

Personals

Love Shack

Another way of finding someone on AOL is to use the Personal Ads, which you'll find by visiting AOL Keyword: **Love Shack**. Love Shack is an area where you can post an advert saying what sort of people you'd like to meet, whether it's for friendship, chatting, romance, or something more.

As well as placing personals, you can also flirt or chat in the message boards and chat rooms – so perhaps it could be the ideal place to go if you want advice on how best to charm the person of your dream via email.

White Pages

So far, the things we've talked about show you how to track down people who are AOL members – and while there are over 33 million of them around the world, sooner or later you might be wanting to find someone who isn't a member.

Maybe you're trying to track down a relative, or look up the phone number for someone in another country. You might be curious about what happened to that person who sat next to you in lectures at university.

People Finder

You can find the answers easily using AOL's White Pages service, which is at AOL Keyword: **People Finder**. All you need to do is type in as much information as you have, click **Find**, then wait while the search is performed. With luck, you'll find plenty of people, including the one that you're looking for, with their address and telephone number and sometimes an email address too.

Are you a bit shy about phoning someone up after too many years? Well, in some countries, you'll see a link next to the results of the search, letting you send them a card. Click on it, and you can type a short message which will be printed on a card and delivered through the post, so you can tell them your email address and see if they get in touch!

Don't worry if you can't find the people you want when you search through AOL's People Finder – there are also lots of other Web pages on the Internet that perform similar functions. Some of them are based on phone directories, while some provide email searches. In the UK, there's a great Web site called Friends Reunited, where you can enter the details of the schools you went to, and the years you were there, to try and contact your contemporaries. Just type **www.friendsreunited.co.uk** into AOL's Keyword box to get started.

Even if you're not looking for someone else, it's a good idea to visit some of the White Pages sites on the Internet, since you can often add your own details – which means people looking for you will be able to track you down more easily.

Genealogy

There's yet another way you can try and track people down, if it's relatives you're after. Go to AOL Keyword: **Genealogy** and you'll find plenty of tips and tricks to trace family members. So if you're not even sure where someone might be living, this could be a good way to get on their trail, through records of marriages, births, and deaths.

However you find people, wherever they are, it'll take only a few moments to send them an email via AOL and establish contact. So, now that you have an idea of how to find family, friends, or people with similar interests, let's take a look at how to use AOL's email system to get in touch.

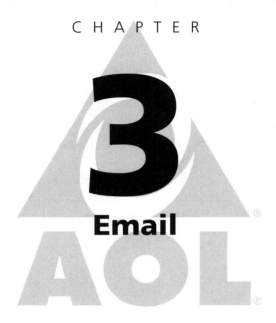

CHAPTER

3

Email

Email is one of the most useful tools ever devised, and with AOL you can send messages to people all over the world, both other AOL subscribers and anyone who has an Internet email address.

First of all, what's an email address? Well, when you signed up to AOL, you chose a screen name for yourself, something like NigelwUK. Your email address is just that, with @aol.com on the end.

The part after the @ is called the domain, and it tells the email system where to send a message – you'll find addresses like news@bbc.co.uk, or tony@number-10.gov.uk. And you can send email to those addresses just as easily as if you were sending it to other AOL members.

When you're sending email to another AOL member, you can save time by missing out the @aol.com part of the address, and just typing their screen name – AOL will deliver the message to them whichever way you type the address.

So, you have an email address – what are you going to do with it?

Well, you can exchange simple messages – email is often much more informal than a written letter – asking people if they want to come to dinner, or enquiring about a product you've seen on their Web site.

Or you can emphasise the important parts of your message by using things like bold text, or colours. Yep, you could even write your Internet letters in green ink if you like!

If you're sending a party invitation by email, for example, you could add colour, or make the important details, like the date and venue, bold and centre them on the screen.

And for even more flair, why not include pictures in your email?

If you've started to talk with someone on AOL and you like the way they sound, you can send a picture to them via email, or you could send photographs of your new pet to your sister on the other side of the world – and you can send files via email to people who aren't on AOL too!

Of course, you don't just have to use AOL mail for fun. You can find it just as useful for work – why not send a client an invoice that they can open in their word processor? Or perhaps you want to work at home with some files from the office. No problem – just send them by email, and they'll be ready for you to download when you get home.

Using AOL mail

It all sounds pretty great, doesn't it? So, let's see how you actually use all these features.

First, let's see how to read your mail – when you sign up with AOL, you'll be automatically sent a welcome message.

Fig. 3.1   The AOL main screen, with new mail showing.

When you sign on to AOL, you'll hear a voice telling you if you have new mail, and you can click **You Have Email** on the opening screen.

Even if you don't have new mail, you can still open your mailbox by clicking **Read Mail** on the AOL toolbar. You can also use the shortcut Ctrl-R to read your mail.

When the mailbox opens, you'll see that it's divided into three sections, called New Mail, Old Mail and Sent Mail.

When someone sends you a message, it appears in the New Mail area, a little like the picture opposite.

All you have to do to read a message is double-click it.

After you've read a message, it's automatically moved to the Old Mail area, where you'll be able to read it again later if you like.

Fig. 3.2 Your mailbox, with new mail waiting.

Mail in the Old Mail area is only kept on AOL for about a week. After that, it's deleted, and you won't be able to access it again. If you want to keep messages longer, you need to save them on your computer, in your Personal Filing Cabinet – read how later in this chapter.

The Sent Mail area of your mailbox is where you can see copies of messages that you've written to other people – and if you think you said something you shouldn't have done in a message to another AOL member, you can even Unsend the message, before they've had time to look at it. Just click to highlight the message, then click **Unsend** at the bottom of the window. Try doing that with the Royal Mail!

When you double-click on a message, it opens in a new window on your screen. At the top of the message, you'll see the name of the person who sent it to you, the date and time it was sent, and the subject.

If you decide after reading the message that you won't be needing it again, just click **Delete** at the bottom of the window, and it's history!

You can simply close the window when you're done, and the message will be transferred to the Old Mail area of your mailbox, or you might decide that you'd like to reply to it – after all, that's usually the point of an email, isn't it?

When you click **Reply**, you'll see another window open, which is just the same as the one that appears when you decide to write a new email, but with the address and subject already filled in for you. You can also add the person's address to your address book by clicking **Add Address**. You can find out more about using the address book later on in this chapter.

Now, let's have a look at writing an email – it really is so simple you'll have the hang of it in no time.

*Before you get too carried away with writing lots of emails, it's a good idea to review the Online Guidelines, which are in **Chapter 10, Online Guidelines**.*

10 Common sense

When you click **Write Email** (or press Ctrl-E on a PC, Command-E on a Mac), you'll see a screen like this one appear.

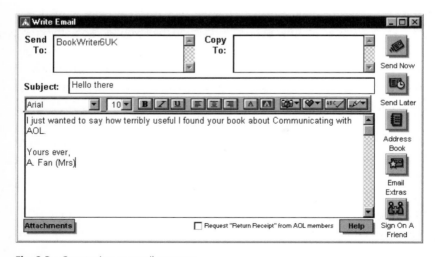

Fig. 3.3 Composing an email message.

As we said, if you've clicked **Reply** after reading a message that someone else sent you, some of the parts of this screen will have been filled in already.

If you're writing a new message, however, you'll need to fill in the address, by clicking in the area labelled **To** and typing the email address of the person you're trying to contact.

Next, click in the **Subject** area, and type a short description. It's best to make it reasonably descriptive, but not too long, so people can decide when they see the subject of the message in their inbox if they want to read it right away.

When you've done that, all you have to do is click in the main area of the window, and type the text of your message.

Remember that email doesn't have to be formal – you'll very rarely see an email beginning Dear Sir, or even Dear Fred; it's much more common just to start with Hi. So don't be too shocked if people seem more familiar than you may be used to when they send you messages.

When you're done, all you have to do is click **Send**, and your message is on its way. If you're sending it to another AOL member, in fact it's probably already got there. And if the person you're writing to is on the Internet, then the message will usually arrive within a few minutes, ready for the next time they sign on and check their email.

Email is so quick that it can sometimes spread like wildfire – you send a message to someone, and they write back a couple of minutes later, and then you reply to them, and so on. You can quickly go from just a short "hello" to knowing a lot more about people – but remember that you don't have to reply to every message that comes your way. If you did, you'd probably be drowning under a sea of email within a few days of joining AOL!

More than words

Everyone's familiar with the old saying that a picture tells a thousand words, and the same can be just as true of an email.

You don't have to restrict yourself to just plain old words.

When you're writing an email, you'll have noticed these buttons along the top of the message area.

Fig. 3.4   Tools and options in the message compose window.

The first few work just like the formatting buttons and tools you have in your word processor program – just highlight some of the text in your message, and then click to make it bold, or change the size or colour.

At the right are two other buttons, for adding a link – the one with a picture of a heart – or a picture – via the camera button – to your email.

A link is just a piece of text that the recipient of the email can click to visit a Web site or, if they're a member, another area of AOL.

You might, for example, send people a link to a Web site that shows a map with your house on it. Or if you know that one of your AOL friends is fond of classic cars, you might send them a link to the classic car area on AOL.

To add a link you first need to go to the place you want to tell your friend about, and look for the **Favourite Places** icon – that's the small heart that appears in the top right of the window. Click on the heart, and a box will appear giving you the option of adding the place to a new email message. And if you've already started writing a message, you can choose **Copy to Clipboard** from the menu that pops up, then click in your email message and choose **Paste** on the **Edit** menu. You can also use the heart icon at the top of the email window to add a place that's already in your own list of Favourites.

If you want to add a picture to your email, just click the camera button, select **Insert a picture**, and choose the picture from your computer's hard disk. It'll be inserted into the message, just where you've finished typing. You can also use a picture as a background, so your text appears on top of it – but remember that could make it hard to see; the other option on the camera button allows you to add a text file from your computer's hard disk. So if you have, for example, the agenda for a club meeting, you can just add it from your computer's disk to save typing it in again.

AOL can automatically change the size of your pictures so that they fit in email – the first time you try to add a picture, you'll see this message, and you can choose whether or not you want the size changed, and if you want to be asked again.

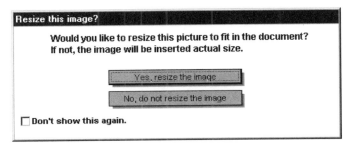

Fig. 3.5   The message resize dialogue box.

You should make sure that the pictures you want to send to people have been saved in the JPEG format. You can send pictures in other formats, but they will take longer to transfer from your computer to AOL, and longer for the recipient to download.

You don't have to put a picture right in the middle of your message – you can also attach it instead.

The difference is a little like either gluing a photo to the page, and putting writing round it, or simply stapling it to the sheet of paper.

Files that you attach to email don't just have to be pictures – you could attach a word processor file, or a sound that you've recorded with your PC. In fact, you can send any type of file that you like.

All you have to do is click **Attachments**, which you'll see at the bottom of the window when you're creating a new message, and then choose the file that you want to send.

You can click **Attachments** more than once, too, if you want to send a whole group of files at the same time.

If you're sending pictures to people on the Internet, rather than other AOL members, you should attach them rather than including them in your message, since not all email programs can understand embedded pictures. Some of the other fancy features of AOL email, like coloured or stylised text may not show up in some other email programs, so don't assume that your recipient will always see the message exactly as you wrote it.

Addresses and the address book

One of the most useful things about email is that it doesn't have to be one to one – you can send the same message to lots of people at the same time, so it's great for things like telling your family the latest news, or inviting a load of friends round to your place for a barbecue.

You can type more than one address in the **Send To** box when you write an email, or you can add extra addresses in the **Copy To** box.

When you receive a message that's been sent to lots of people, you'll see that as well as a **Reply** button, there's also **Reply All**. If you use **Reply All**, your reply will automatically be sent to all the same people as the original.

There's another way you can include people in a message, called Bcc, or Blind Carbon Copy. That means that the addresses you use as Bcc addresses won't be visible to any of the other recipients of the message.

Why would you want to do that? Well, perhaps you're writing to a company to complain about their products, and you want to send a copy to a friend, so that they can see what you've written. Just add your friend as a Bcc address, and they'll receive a copy too.

To add a Bcc address, all you need to do is type the address in the **Copy To** box at the head of the email, but put brackets round it.

If you're organising a surprise party and don't want anyone to know who else is coming, write a new message addressed to yourself, and put all the real recipients' addresses in brackets, so that they are all Bccs – that way no one will know who you have mailed.

Of course, it's important to remember that just because you *can* send email to lots of people at the same time, it's not always a good idea.

In particular, you should never send unsolicited commercial emails, or pass on chain emails to other people. And be very cautious before you send files to lots of people via email.

AOL's email has an address book which you can use to keep track of the addresses of people you want to write to, to save you the trouble of remembering them all.

All you need to do is click **Address Book** when you're composing a message, and choose the names that you want to add to your message.

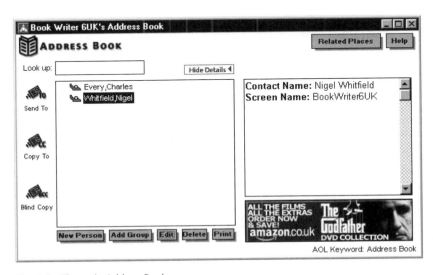

Fig. 3.6 The main Address Book screen.

As you can see, the address book lists all the addresses that you've saved, and you just need to pick them from the list on the right, or type in enough information to look someone up. Then click **Send To** to add them as a recipient of an email, or **Copy To** or **Blind Copy** to add them as a secondary recipient.

You can group people in the address book, so all your work colleagues are together, for example, or family addresses are listed together.

To add a new entry, just click **New Person**.

The Contact Details screen is where you fill in the details of the person you want to add. The important things to enter on this screen are the addresses, which you should put in either the **Email 1** or **Email 2** boxes. You don't have to fill in any of the other information, but if you do, then you can use the address book to look up information like postal addresses or phone numbers – you'll see spaces for adding that info when you click the tabs along the top of the contact details screen.

AOL automatically synchronises your address book for you, which means that if you connect to AOL from a friend's computer using the AOL software, you'll have all your contact information at your fingertips.

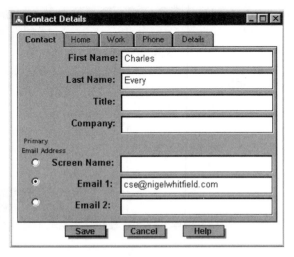

Fig. 3.7 The Contact Details screen.

When you send an email using the address book, AOL will usually choose the address you enter in the **Email 1** box, so remember to put the one that you use most in that box.

Group emails

The address book can save you a lot of time, but if you're sending a message to a lot of people, there could still be a lot of clicking.

Fortunately, there is another way. If you have groups of people that you regularly exchange messages with – for example colleagues, family, or an amateur football team, you can use Groups@AOL to save you all the hard work.

You can read more about groups in *Chapter 7, Groups and Web Sites*, including how to set them up and how to use the Group email facility.

7 Groups@AOL

Group email gives you a single address that you can send a message to and it'll be automatically distributed to all the other members of the Group – so you don't have to worry about forgetting someone.

So, if you find you're often sending a message to the same selection of people, take a look at AOL's Groups facility. It could save you a lot of time – and there are plenty of other cool features too.

When you're reading your emails, keep an eye on the Buddy List window. AOL will automatically tell you if the email contacts whose messages you're reading are online, so you can contact them quickly using the AOL Instant Messenger™ service and get the answer you need right away, instead of checking your email later. You can read more about the Buddy List feature and how to send an Instant Message in Chapter 4, Instant Message.

4 Instant Message

Organising your email

So far, we've just looked at the email that you see when you connect to AOL, which is stored in your New Mail, Old Mail and Sent Mail boxes. But what happens if you want to keep messages for longer than the week that they stay in Old Mail?

If you're in the middle of a long email discussion with someone, you might want to keep the messages – they could be useful if there's any confusion later about who said what, for example.

Or maybe you've received such a sweet Valentine's Day note from your partner that you want to keep it forever.

No problem – your Personal Filing Cabinet, or PFC, is the place to store all the messages that you want to keep.

When you open your mailbox and view the list of messages, click **Save to PFC**, and the message will be transferred to your computer so that you can read it long after it would have disappeared from your AOL mailbox.

If you want to keep copies of all the mail you send and receive au-tomatically, click **Preferences** *on the* **Customise** *menu on the AOL toolbar, and on the Personal Filing Cabinet screen, make sure the options for* **Retain all email I read** *and* **Retain all email I send** *are checked.*

You can access messages that you have saved this way by clicking **Personal Filing Cabinet** on the **Email** menu. The screen you'll see looks something like Fig. 3.8, with sections for incoming email, mail you've sent, and mail waiting to be sent.

Tidying up your messages
Once you've been using AOL for a while, especially if you choose the option to automatically keep copies of your messages, you'll have quite a lot of

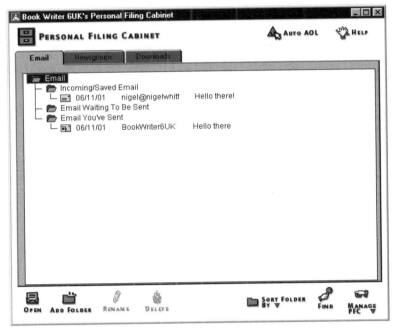

Fig. 3.8 The Personal Filing Cabinet (PFC) email screen.

messages in the list, and it'll be pretty hard to find the one you're looking for.

When that happens – or before – it's time to tidy up your messages. As you can see, when you're reading offline email, there's a button at the bottom of the screen that's labelled **Add Folder**.

It works a little like the New Folder option when you're browsing your computer's hard disk. Click it, and you'll be asked for the name of the folder – you might want one, say, for your sports club. Type the name, and the folder will appear in the list of messages.

Now you can just click to select the messages you want to move, and drag them all into the new folder.

Of course, you probably want to keep all the messages you've exchanged with someone in the same folder, whether they're from you or to you. It's easy! You can move incoming and outgoing email to any of the folders, just by dragging it. And you can make as many folders as you like, so why not have one for each project you're involved in, or for each of your best friends?

If you read your messages from another computer, they won't be saved on your hard disk, so remember to either mark them as unread, by clicking **Keep as new***, or save them to your PFC manually next time you read mail on your own computer.*

Speeding up email

OK, so now you've added your friends to your address book, and organised your Personal Filing Cabinet so that you can find messages easily, whether they're from the other members of the local Neighbourhood Watch or your old schoolfriend in Alabama.

But once you start sending and receiving a lot of mail – especially if you're swapping pictures with the family, or sending work back to the office – you'll probably get a bit tired of waiting for everything to download, or for the files that you're sending to upload to AOL.

You can take care of that too. When you're writing an email, you'll see that there's a **Send Later** button as well as a **Send** one. Just click that, and it'll be added to a list of waiting emails.

Free up your phone line by writing emails before you connect to AOL. The **Send** *button will be dimmed, since you can't use it, but you'll still be able to click* **Send Later***.*

You can send all the waiting emails in one go by clicking **Email waiting to be sent** on the **Email** menu. Click **Send all**, and you'll see a bar showing the progress of all the messages – and you can even click a check box to tell AOL to disconnect you automatically when all the mail has been sent, so you can get on with something else right away.

AOL can collect your messages for you in one go too, using a feature called Automatic AOL. There's not enough space in this book to cover it in detail, but it's very easy to use. Just choose **Setup Automatic AOL** from the **Email** button, and follow the simple instructions on the screen.

You can even tell your computer to dial up and collect messages automatically at the same time each day, while you're on holiday!

By now you should know just about all you need to know about emails, so let's take a look at another of the cool ways of communicating with AOL – Instant Message.

4

Instant Message

Email may be a great way of keeping in touch with friends and colleagues, and it's certainly fast – but these days, we all sometimes crave a little more speed. You can pick up the phone and ask someone a question if you're in a hurry, but wouldn't it be a great idea if you could do the same online, even if the other person is half way around the world?

The solution is the AOL Instant Messenger™ service. When you send an email, you're never sure if it's been read, or if a reply is on its way – which can be pretty frustrating at times, not least when you've just invited someone for a romantic dinner!

With Instant Message, you know right away that your message has appeared on someone else's screen, because you can't send it unless they're connected. And if they need to reply, they just click a button, and their response appears on your screen within a couple of seconds.

Even more useful, the Buddy List feature allows AOL to show you a list of all the people you usually exchange messages with, and tell you which of your

friends is online at the same time as you, so you can just click on their name
and send a message.

Getting started with Instant Message

Sooner or later, when you start using AOL, you'll receive your first Instant Message, or IM. Unless you've told a friend your screen name already, it might be
from a complete stranger, just saying hello. When an IM arrives, it appears on
the screen in a new window, like this.

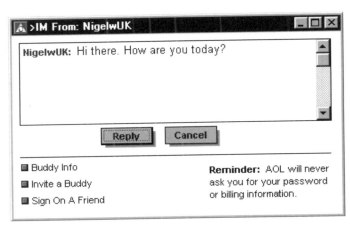

Fig. 4.1   An incoming Instant Message.

If you click **Cancel**, then the message will disappear. But if you'd like to reply,
just click **Reply**, type your response in the bottom box, then click **Send**.

> *You can also press* **Enter** *on the number keypad to send your message*
> *on a PC, or Apple-Return on a Macintosh.*

In just a couple of seconds, your response will appear on the other person's
screen, and you'll both be seeing the same – all the comments in the order
they were made, with the Screen Name of the person who typed at the beginning of the line.

It really is that simple to reply to a message you've been sent – and it's just as simple to send a message to someone if you know their Screen Name. All you need to do is press Ctrl-I on a PC, or Apple-I on a Macintosh, then type in the name of the person you want to reach, and your message.

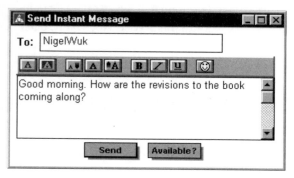

Fig. 4.2   Sending an Instant Message.

If you're not sure whether or not someone is online, you can click **Available** at the bottom, instead of typing, and if the person is online, you'll see a message telling you that you can send Instant Messages to them.

An important message

From time to time, you may receive messages from people claiming to work for AOL, and asking for your password or billing information, such as credit card details. They may even say that your account with AOL will be terminated if you don't respond. No matter how convincing their request may seem, you should not reply.

AOL staff will never ask for passwords or billing information via an Instant Message or email. If you ever receive such a message – and sadly there are people out there who will try anything to get your credit card number – go to AOL Keyword: **Notify AOL***.*

Finding out more about who's messaged you

Click **Buddy Info** at the bottom of an IM screen to see more about a person. If you choose **View Profile**, AOL will fetch the profile of the person who sent you the message – if they have one – so you can find out a little bit about them.

You can read how to make your own Profile, so that people can find out about you, in *Chapter 2, Family and Friends*. It's a good idea to make one as soon as you feel comfortable with going online, since many people won't reply to your messages if you don't have a Profile giving at least basic details about yourself. Think of your Profile as a little like the introductions a host will give at a party – without them, some people will think you a little rude just launching into a conversation.

2 Profiles

Spicing up your Instant Messages

Instant Messages aren't just plain text. Along the top of the area where you type your message, you'll see a set of buttons that you can use to add different typefaces, or choose a different colour to type in. You can make the letters bigger or smaller, and if you click on the **Smiley** icon you can choose one of a range, rather than having to type them in yourself.

You can even add a link to an Instant Message, so that the person you're talking with can just click on the link and go directly to a page that you want to show them.

If you have a site or a section of AOL saved in your Favourites, you can just drag the heart icon from your Favourite Places into the IM window, and it'll be inserted automatically. Or you can click **Insert Link** on the **Edit** menu, and then type the details of the link that you want to send into the boxes provided.

You might be worried about links being sent to your children or other family members, that could direct them to unsuitable material. If you are, you can automatically prevent links in Instant Messages from working for them. You can read how in **Chapter 10, Online Guidelines***.*

10 Restricting Instant Messages

Instant Messages and the Internet

When you sign up to AOL, you're joining a community of over 33 million people around the world. You might think that will provide enough people to talk with, but there are even more.

When you connect to AOL, you can also exchange Instant Messages with users of the AOL Instant Messenger™ service, or AIM. AIM is a free service that is available to anyone with an Internet connection, anywhere in the world – so if you have friends or colleagues who don't connect to the Net through AOL, why not encourage them to use AIM, so you can swap messages with them?

You can find out more about AIM, including how your friends can use it, in **Chapter 9, AOL Anywhere***.*

9 AIM

When you first receive a message from an AIM user, you'll probably see a screen asking you if you want to accept a message, and telling you the name of the person who sent it.

It's called Knock-Knock, and it's designed to give you a little extra protection before accepting messages from the Internet, since there aren't handy Profiles where you can look up information about the people messaging you. Just click **Yes** to accept the message, or **No** if you don't want to accept it – the person who tried to send it won't be able to send any more to you. Handy if it's the boss trying to find out how ill you are!

You can turn off the Knock-Knock feature from AOL's Instant Message Preferences screen, which is reached via the **My AOL** menu.

The Buddy List feature

Instant Message is a great way to keep in touch with people, but if you had to try sending a message just to find out if someone was online, that would be pretty annoying, wouldn't it?.

That's where your Buddy List window comes in. It's a small window on your computer screen that tells you when the people you've added are online, so you can send them a message right away.

A Buddy List window will appear when you sign on to AOL; if it doesn't, or if you've closed the window, you can call it up with the AOL Keyword: **Buddy View**, or by clicking **Buddy List** on the **People** menu, then **View**.

Fig. 4.3 The Buddy List display.

As you can see, the Buddy List window has three entries in it, called Buddies, Family and Co-Workers; next to each name is a pair of numbers in brackets. To start with, they'll all say 0/0; the names are groups of buddies and the first number is the number of people in that group who are online at the moment. The second number is the total number in the group.

Grouping your buddies makes it easier to remember who's who, or just to keep an eye on a certain selection of people. If you're interested in cars, for example, why not make a new group called Car people, and put some of your new online buddies in there? Then you can see right away if there's someone to talk engines with when you sign on.

When there are people online in a group, you'll see a little + sign next to the group name; click it to see the names of the people in the group, or to close the group and just see its title, if you don't want to be distracted by seeing when someone comes online.

Using the Buddy List feature

Of course, a Buddy List group with no buddies in it isn't very useful at all, so to get started, click **Setup**, and a screen like this will appear.

Fig. 4.4 Setting up your Buddy List group.

To add a new buddy to your list, click on the group that you want to add them to, then click **New Person**. Type in the Screen Name that you want to add, and press **Enter**. You'll see them appear in the list on the left of this screen.

Don't worry if you accidentally added someone to the wrong group – you can just click on a name and drag it into another one.

You can also add new groups, or rename any of the existing ones – perhaps you don't think you'll be using AOL to send Instant Messages to colleagues, so you could click **Co-Workers**, then click **Rename** and change the name of the group to something more useful, like Rangers Fans. You can add as many groups as you like.

When you've finished, click **Done** and your Buddy List window will update to show the new buddies and groups that you've added.

Remember that your Buddy List window can show you whether or not your friends on the Internet are connected to the AOL Instant Messenger service too, so don't forget to add their AIM screen names as well.

Once you've put people in your Buddy List groups, the feature starts to become much more useful. You can send an Instant Message to someone just by double clicking on their name. The usual Instant Message screen will appear, with the name filled in for you. Just type your message and click **Send**.

Info can be used to see where your buddy is on AOL – it lets you know if they're in a chat room, and gives you the choice of going straight to the same chat room, so you can join them in telling jokes, flirting, or swapping tips on tuning up a 1982 Ford Escort.

The middle button, **Chat**, sends a special sort of Instant Message, which is an invitation to a chat room. If you select a group, it will send an invitation to all the members of that group – so you could just select your Family group and have a little online reunion if you want to tell them all about your new job at the same time.

If you select a name, just that name will be filled in on the invitation screen, which looks like this.

Fig. 4.5 Inviting your buddies to chat.

You can add extra names, up to a total of 22, in the box at the top of this screen, and customise the message if you like. When you click **Send Now**, everyone will receive an invitation – including you. To join the chat, just click **Go** on the invitation, and wait for everyone else to come into the room, then start chatting.

Buddy preferences

You can alter some of the preferences for the Buddy List feature; choose **Setup** and then click **Settings**. You can use the different tabs on this screen to control how the Buddy List feature and Instant Message works on your computer.

The first screen, Buddy List, allows you to select sounds that will be played when buddies sign on, so you can be doing something else on the computer and you'll hear when a friend arrives. If you select to have the Mail Contacts group displayed, then AOL will automatically add a new group with that title, whenever you're reading your mail online.

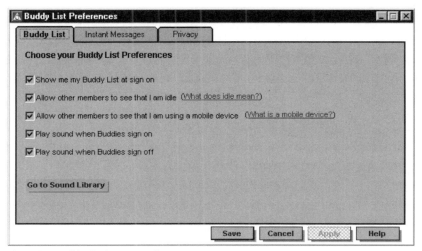

Fig. 4.6   Buddy List feature settings.

That way, if someone you've just sent mail to or read mail from is online, you'll see right away, so you can send them a quick message like "I hope that date is ok – can you confirm it now?" without having to wait for a response via email.

On the IM screen you can choose options including a timestamp on messages, so you know when they arrived if you're away from the computer. You can even add a special icon to show on someone's screen when you send them a message.

If you're on holiday, or perhaps taking a day sick at home, you might not want your boss to see if you're online, but you still want other people to be able to talk to you. Or maybe you want to hide from your teacher, so they can't remind you to do your homework.

The Privacy settings let you create a list of people and set preferences, which can apply just to the Buddy List feature or to both the Buddy List feature and Instant Message.

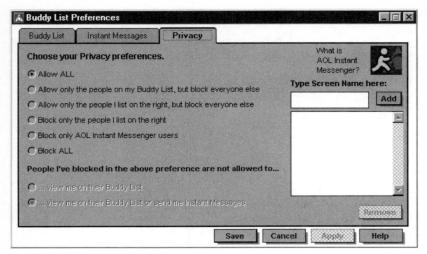

Fig. 4.7 Privacy settings screen.

For example, you could block people in the list from your Buddy List group, which means that they won't be able to tell when you're online, but they could still send you an Instant Message.

Or you could allow only the people in the list to see you in their Buddy List group and exchange Instant Messages – you might use this option, for example, to create a list of people that your children can swap messages with, including grandparents, classmates, and teachers.

Choose the option that suits the level of privacy that you want – and remember to check how it uses the list of names that you've entered. Some of the options block everyone on the list, while others only allow people who are listed to contact you.

If you'd like to block messages completely for your child's AOL Screen Name, you should use the Parental Controls feature, which they won't be able to alter. You can read about it in **Chapter 10, Online Guidelines***.*

10 Keeping in control

Once you've started using it, you'll wonder how you ever managed without Instant Message – and perhaps you'll wonder how you can survive when you're away from your computer.

AOL has plenty of different ways that you can carry on accessing Instant Message, even when you don't have access to a computer with the AOL software on it. You can read about how to access Instant Message from other PCs, in a cybercafé or even on a Palm organiser in **Chapter 9, AOL Anywhere**. For now, though, let's go on and see how you can communicate with other AOL users in chat rooms.

9 AOL Anywhere

5

Chat Rooms

The ways of communicating that we've looked at so far are, on the whole, just ways for two people to swap information. And, of course, they're ideally suited to communicating with people you already know.

If you're new to online communication, though, how will you find people to talk with? AOL's chat rooms are one answer – and contrary to what you might think, chat rooms aren't full of people with no social life, or those just looking for seedy encounters. The vast majority of chat rooms are full of ordinary people, just like you, passing the time, and getting to know each other, or having discussions – both heated and otherwise.

Think of a chat room as a little like a pub; each one that you visit has its own regulars and a unique atmosphere. You can wander in and strike up a conversation with someone, or just say "Hello." Sometimes, it's just fun to sit in your corner with a pint and watch how everyone else interacts, until you have a feel for the place. Or perhaps one of the regulars will come over and say hello to you.

An AOL chat room really does work in just the same way – and there's even the equivalent of the landlord and his staff, in the form of Guides and Hosts, to welcome newcomers and make sure that no one gets out of order.

If you want to know some of the basic ground rules, why not take a look at Chapter 10, Online Guidelines? You can also read a little more about Guides and Hosts.

10 Online Guidelines

There is one big difference between chat rooms and a pub though – in a pub, you might have to ask around until you find someone who knows about cars, or tips on travelling to a particular country.

Chat rooms make it much easier, since you can go to a chat room dedicated to a specific topic, such as cars, current affairs, or lonely hearts. Sure, you could go to a singles night at your local bar, but we've not found a pub that's exclusively full of car enthusiasts yet!

Because they're usually dedicated to a specific topic, you can use chat rooms for all sorts of things. Not sure what's wrong with your computer? Go to one of the more technical chat rooms, and perhaps you'll find someone who's already solved the problem you're experiencing.

Or maybe you want to practise your French before going on holiday. AOL is international, and you can join a French chat room too

Perhaps you just want to vent your anger about global warming and its dangers, in which case you might find people talking about it in the current affairs chat area.

AOL Live

There's even more too, with AOL Keyword: **AOL Live**, where you can talk online to famous people, whether celebrities from the showbusiness world, or politicians, putting your questions over the computer so that they can give you a response right away.

And, of course, going into a chat room can be liberating for people who are hard of hearing, or unable to speak face to face. Instead of being restricted to using sign language or lip reading – which can be hard when the other person isn't used to it – in a chat room everyone is equal. As long as you can type, your voice can be heard.

There are plenty of reasons, then, to use chat rooms, so let's get a move on and see how you can find places to chat on AOL.

Finding chat rooms

If you look round AOL's channels, you'll find plenty of chat rooms, covering all sorts of topics. The channels each cover a broad area, like Technology, Local Life, Health, and so on. Just pick one from the AOL **Channel** menu, and browse through to find a section that you're interested in.

In most of the areas, you'll find plenty of chat rooms; all you have to do is click the appropriate button to take you into one.

If you don't want to spend ages hunting round AOL to find a chat room, just click Chat and Communities on AOL's channel bar, which will show you a list of all the chat rooms and message areas for all AOL's different communities. Just pick one from the list, and you'll be chatting in no time at all.

Quick Chat

If you simply want a list of all the chat rooms – perhaps you know the name of a room, but can't remember how to get there – then try AOL Keyword: **Quick Chat**. The Quick Chat screen lists all the main chat rooms provided on AOL UK.

Fig. 5.1 Chat and Communities screen.

*You can stop your children from accessing chat rooms by using the Parental Controls, described in **Chapter 10, Online Guidelines**.*

10 Keeping in control

Using chat rooms

News Chat

Figure 5.2 shows a chat room – we've chosen News Chat, which you can also reach directly with the AOL Keyword: **News Chat**.

As you can see, the top of the window shows the name of the room that you're in, and down the left you can see a list of all the people who are presently in the room with you. To the right is the main chat room window, while at the bottom of the screen is a blank area where you can type your comments.

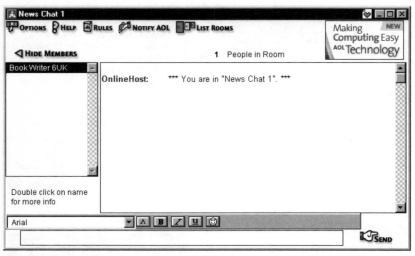

Fig. 5.2 The News Chat room.

Type a quick message like **Hello there** and either click **Send** or press **Enter** to send it. You'll see it appear in the main part of the chat room window, with your name at the start of the line.

As other people talk, their comments will appear at the bottom of the screen, and eventually the first comments you saw will disappear off the top, as new ones appear below – but if you're having a discussion and want to check what you said a while ago, you can just scroll back and read it again.

If you want more space to see the comments that are being made, just click on the triangle labelled **Hide Members** at the top of the screen and the list of people will disappear. Click again, and it'll reappear.

Members with names beginning GuideUK or UKHost are AOL volunteers, available to help and guide you as you use chat rooms or other parts of AOL. If they tell you to do something, you should always listen!

Although the actual chat is probably what you're in the room for, the member list is one of the most useful parts of the chat room – it's your key to making friends online, and finding out more about the people you're talking with.

The member list and chat options

It's a good idea to sit and watch a chat room for a little while – you can see who is making the sort of comments you agree with, or who you might want to avoid. And, of course, you'll get an idea of what the current discussion is all about.

But really, you probably want to know about the people who are there too.

When you joined the room, you probably noticed a message from OnlineHost, telling you you'd joined, and you may have seen some others since then, letting you know when people join and leave the room. OnlineHost is the AOL computer, and the messages help you keep track of who's in the room.

Click **Options** at the top of the chat room window, and you can choose whether or not to see the messages when people join and leave the room – and you can also have the member list in alphabetical order, which many people find easier to read.

OK, so someone's made an incredibly witty comment, or mentioned that they live in the same town as you – how do you make contact?

Well, you can just type a message into the chat room window, and see if they respond. Remember to include the Screen Names of the members you're responding to, so they know you're talking to them. In a busy chat room, though, it's not always easy to keep track of everything that's being said. Sometimes, it's like there are five or six different conversations going on at the same time.

Why not find out a bit more about someone, and perhaps send them an Instant Message? All you have to do is double click their name in the list of members, and a small window will pop up, giving you the option of viewing their Profile, or sending an Instant Message.

Start by viewing their Profile, and after a couple of moments, AOL will pull up the information that they entered about themselves. If you don't have a Profile of your own, now is a good time to make one – you can find out how in **Chapter 2, Friends and Family**.

2 Profiles

If you like the Profile, all you need to do is click **Send an Instant Message**, type your message, and you're away. And if nothing in the Profile takes your interest, no matter – there are plenty of other people you can find to chat to.

Chatting

Chat rooms cover all sorts of topics, and you'll often find people being much more candid than they would be if you met them in your local pub for the first time.

Like email, chat rooms are very informal, and people will often share all sorts of information – but remember that you don't have to do anything if you don't want to. If someone else is talking about their problems, for example, and you'd rather not tell everyone that you've been through the same thing, why not send them an Instant Message to let them know how you coped? Or maybe you want to share with someone else your support for the political party that everyone else is criticising?

Whatever the reason, using Instant Message is a great way to get to know someone a bit better after you've seen an interesting comment in a chat room.

While you're talking in the main chat room, you can still use the same effects, such as coloured letters or fancy typefaces, that you have available in Instant Message or email; just use the font list and the style buttons above the area where you type.

You can type a couple of lines of text at a time into a chat room – AOL will beep when you can't type any more. So if you have a long comment to make, split it up into chunks – otherwise it's a bit like talking all the time and not letting anyone else get a word in edgeways.

It's considered bad form to type lots of very short comments just to fill up the chat room window and scroll messages by other people off the top of the screen.

More chat options

As well as the **Options** button, you'll notice a few others at the top of the chat room screen: **Help, Rules, Notify AOL** and **List Rooms**.

The first gives you a little guidance on how to use chat rooms and how they work, while **Rules** will take you to a section where you can check the AOL Conditions of Service.

Trouble

Use **Notify AOL** to call for assistance – for example, if someone's being really abusive in a chat room, or deliberately disrupting it, you can use this button to call for a Guide or Host to help out. The screen that appears is the same one you'll see at AOL Keyword: **Trouble**. You can read more about getting help in *Chapter 10, Online Guidelines*.

10 Help is at hand

List Rooms works slightly differently depending on which chat room you're in.

For example, if you're in a particularly busy room – rooms are limited to around 40 members – **List Rooms** might display several rooms with identical names, and a number at the end, like News Chat 1, News Chat 2 and so on. These rooms are automatically added by AOL to ensure that plenty of people can chat, without getting too crowded. You can imagine the chaos if 100 people were all typing different things into a chat room – it would be almost impossible to follow any conversations.

Sometimes, when you click to go to a particular chat room, you'll be taken to one of these instead, after AOL displays a message telling you the room is full, asking if you'd like to visit a similar one.

From some other rooms, **List Rooms** will show you a slightly different list, with a set of categories on the left hand side, and all the rooms in that category on the right – this list includes all the rooms on international AOL services, as well as rooms created by members.

When you're looking at a list of rooms, you can either click **Go** to visit the room right away, or **Who's Here**, which will pop up a small window listing the people in that room.

So, if you're looking for a friend that you said you'd meet in a particular room and they're not there, click **List Rooms** to see if AOL's created an overflow room, and use **Who's Here** to see if they're waiting for you in there. You can also use **Locate**, at the bottom of your Buddy List™ window or at the bottom of the Profile screen, to find someone.

Quick Chat

*If you find a chat room that you like, but can't quite remember how you got there, double-click the **Heart** icon at the top right to add it to your Favourite Places, or look for it on the AOL Keyword: **Quick Chat** list.*

Now you know all about chatting in AOL's chat rooms, and how to find them, why not take some time to wander round, popping into the different rooms? You can only be in one chat room at a time – if you keep the Quick Chat window open, just double-click a new room and the chat window you're in will change to reflect the new title.

And, of course, don't forget that you can have a private chat with your buddies too, inviting them from your Buddy List window, as we explained in *Chapter 4, Instant Message*.

4 Using the Buddy List feature

So whether it's meeting new friends in a social chat room, asking for help in a technical area, or planning a party with some buddies, chat on AOL is a great way to get people together.

In **Chapter 8, Help and Advice**, you can read more about using AOL for help and advice. For now, that's all about chat. It's time to have a look at using message boards to communicate with people.

8 Help and Advice

CHAPTER

6

Message Boards

So far we've seen three different ways of communicating with other people via AOL – email, the AOL Instant Messenger™ service, and chat rooms. The first two are essentially a way of communicating with one person at a time, while the last is a great way of sharing things with people, as long as they're connected to AOL at the same time as you are.

Message boards are the fourth main way of communicating with AOL, and they can be one of the liveliest.

A message board is an area where you can write a message, a little like an email, and then post it for everyone to see. All the people who visit the same board will be able to read your message, and reply to it if they want to. The sequence of messages and replies is known as a thread.

Just like when you write an email, you can choose a subject when you post a message. However, to make it easier to find messages you're interested in, message boards are subdivided into topics. You might find, for example, a TV message board with topics for different shows like *Neighbours*, *Coronation*

Street and *Panorama*. All you have to do is choose the most appropriate topic and post your message in it.

Sounds simple, doesn't it? And it is – if you can read and write email messages, you'll have no problems with message boards, though they are a little more complicated.

You can use message boards for all sorts of things – you might find a place to ask if anyone has a killer recipe for guacamole, for example, or perhaps you want to know if anyone can recommend a restaurant that's good for organic food. Maybe you want to ask if anyone else has had problems with a drug that you've been prescribed, or you've read a story from someone about their cat dying, and you think it might help them if you share your experiences of grieving.

Whatever the reason, message boards offer a place for people to joke, flirt, swap stories, and even argue about the hot topics of the day. You'll find message boards all over AOL, and along with chat rooms, they're a great way to meet new people and make online friends.

Once you've started using message boards, it's easy to find yourself checking them regularly, to see if anyone's responded to your witty comment or plea for help. And if you decide that you really do like the conversation in a particular message board, we'll show you later in this chapter how you can tell AOL to automatically download all the new messages for you to read at your leisure, without tying up your phone line.

Getting started with message boards

Message Boards

There are lots of places you could start with message boards – there are discussion areas on all of AOL's channels. You can reach them by clicking **Chat and Communities**, as well as by following links within the different channels. For now, we're going to begin with the Families message board, which is where parents can find tips, messages, and information on various topics. Click **Chat**

and Communities on the channel bar at the left of the screen, and then click the **Message Boards** link. You'll see a screen like this one, listing all the message boards.

Fig. 6.1   The Message Boards list

To visit a message board, just double-click on its name, and you'll be taken right there. All of AOL's message boards work in the same way, so you can look through the list and pick a different one to visit if you like.

The main area of the screen shows the topics in the message board and the number of subjects in each topic. If you want to read the messages in a topic, all you have to do is click one of the first two buttons – **List All** or **List Unread** – after clicking on the topic.

When you click **List All**, AOL will open a new window, showing you all the subjects in the topic, along with the author of the message and the date it was created – and the list will include all the messages from the last 30 days, even if you've read them all – handy if you want to find something you've already seen.

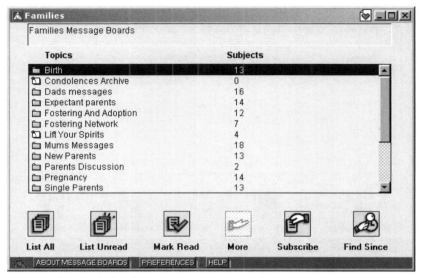

Fig. 6.2   The main folder of the Families Message Board.

It's much more useful to click **List Unread**, which will show you a list of all the messages posted since your last visit; this is the one to click if you want to see who's responded to your own posting, for example, or just to keep on top of the discussions going on.

If you decide that there's nothing in a topic that interests you, click **Mark Read** and AOL will treat all the messages in that topic as if you've read them. If you've been away for a while, this might be a good way to get back on top of the messages, instead of wading through them all.

If **More** is showing, then you can click on it to see extra topics. **Find Since** shows you all the messages since a particular date, and **Subscribe** is used for some of the more advanced message board functions, which we'll cover later on in this chapter.

Reading messages

The first thing to do is to start reading the messages, so click on one of the topics, and you'll see a list of messages. It could look something like Fig. 6.3.

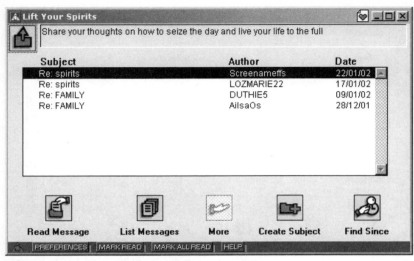

Fig. 6.3   Message board subject listing – non-threaded.

Or it might look like this instead:

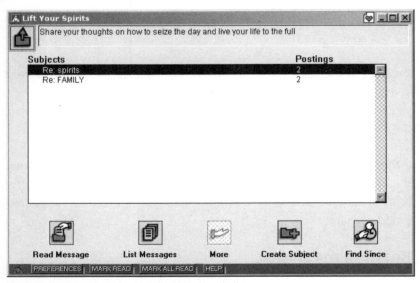

Fig. 6.4   Message board subject listing – threaded.

As you can see, the first listing shows all the individual posts, along with the author and the date they wrote their message. The second listing groups all the messages together, according to their subject and the order in which they were written, just showing you the number of messages on each subject.

Many people find this "threaded" view much easier, because you can be sure you're reading the conversation properly.

To switch between threaded and non-threaded views, click **Preferences** *at the bottom of the message board screens.*

Whichever way you choose to view the messages, you'll see the same buttons along the bottom of the window – **Read Message**, **List Messages**, **More**, **Create Subject** and **Find Since**.

The best thing to do is simply to click **Read Message** after clicking on a subject that interests you – or you can just double-click on the message, and it will open automatically.

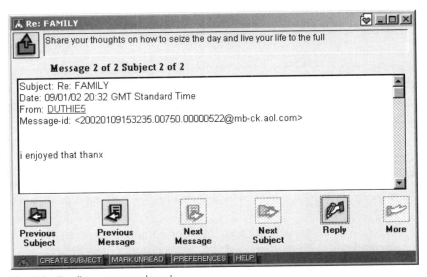

Fig. 6.5   Reading a message board.

When you're reading a message, you'll see buttons at the bottom of the message window for previous and next message, and previous and next subject.

If you're viewing the messages by threads, you can follow the conversation from start to finish (or from wherever it was when you first joined the message board – some threads can go on for weeks!) by clicking **Previous Message** and **Next Message**.

When you get to the end of a thread, the buttons go dim, and you can move to another thread by using the **Previous Subject** and **Next Subject** buttons. Those last two are the only ones that work if you don't look at messages by threads.

Reply, unsurprisingly enough, lets you post a response to someone else's message.

Posting messages

There are two different ways that you can post a message on a message board – you can start a conversation of your own, or you can reply to someone else's message.

If you're looking for help or advice on something specific, it's probably best to create a new subject, so that people can see it easily and reply if they want to. But if you just want to join in a conversation or discussion, then you should probably post a reply to one of the messages you've just read.

Creating a new subject

To create a new subject of your own, just find the message board where you want to say something, and then double-click on the most appropriate topic.

Always pick an appropriate topic for your posting; if you post in the wrong place, you may get fewer responses, and you could upset regular posters to the message board too.

When the list of subjects in the topic appears, click **Create Subject** at the bottom of the screen, and you'll see a blank box like this one appear, with the name of the topic at the top as a reminder.

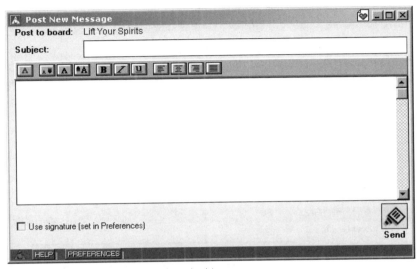

Fig. 6.6 Creating a new message board subject.

Fill in a subject for your message – and make sure it's a meaningful one. If you just put something like "Help" then many people will simply skip past your message, rather than spend time reading it to see if it is an interesting subject. Put something like "How do I cope with pregnancy" or "Ford Cortina 1977 gearbox problems" so that people will know whether or not they have anything useful to say to you.

Just like composing an email, you should type your message in the main part of the screen, and you can use effects like bold, italic, and different colours.

You'll also see an option at the bottom to add a signature. That's a short piece of standard text that you can create by clicking **Preferences**. If you're posting in a forum for car enthusiasts, for example, you might put your real name and the cars you own in the signature. Many people will put a favourite quotation after their name, perhaps giving you an idea of their character.

If you do create a signature, keep it short and simple and avoid using it to advertise your own business – people will soon get annoyed if they have to read an advert for Acme Autos every few messages.

When you've finished creating your message, just click **Send**, and it'll be added to the message board for everyone else to read.

Replying to messages

When you see a message in a message board that strikes a chord with you – perhaps you think you can help the poster, or they live close by – you'll probably want to reply. Or perhaps you should send them an email instead?

Whatever you want to do, just click **Reply** at the bottom of the message, and a screen like this one will pop up.

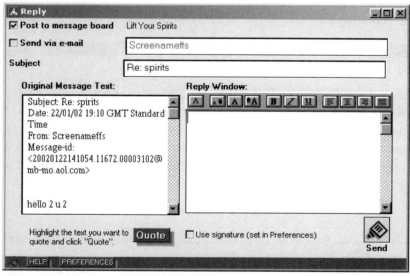

Fig. 6.7 Replying to a message post.

As you can see, at the top of the window there are two check boxes, one for **Post to message board** and one for **Send via email**. You can choose either or both. If you click the **Send via email** box, you can enter an email address

– AOL will have automatically filled in the screen name of the original poster for you.

You can change the subject if you like, though it can be confusing if you change the subject without a good reason.

Often, when people change a subject, they put the old one in brackets, prefixed with the word Was: like "Kathy Beale (Was: Eastenders)"

The area at the right is where you can type your message, and once again you can use effects like bold, coloured, or centred type. To the left, you'll see the text of the message that you're replying to, so that you can read through it if you need to refer to something that the original post said.

Quote (at the bottom) is used to copy parts of the old message into the new one, which some people find a handy trick when they're making points about what someone else has said.

Although quoting can make it easier to follow an argument or discussion, you shouldn't quote any more than you have to. It's considered bad form to quote more than you actually write yourself!

To quote text from the original message, just highlight it in the window on the left, then click **Quote**, and it'll be copied into your own message, preceded by a > symbol, so that readers can see the words are ones that you've included from another message.

When you're happy with the message, just click **Send**, and your message will be posted to the board, emailed or both, depending on the options that you chose.

And that's it – you know how to use message boards to ask questions or take part in discussions.

Message boards for advanced users

My Boards

Once you've stated to get the hang of message boards, you might find that it's a little irksome to have to click through all the different screens to reach your favourite ones.

Of course, you can add them to your Favourite Places, but you'll still have to visit them each in turn, won't you?

Well, no, actually. Remember the **Subscribe** button on the Topics page of each message board? If you click that, the message board will be added to My Boards, which is a sort of message board of message boards.

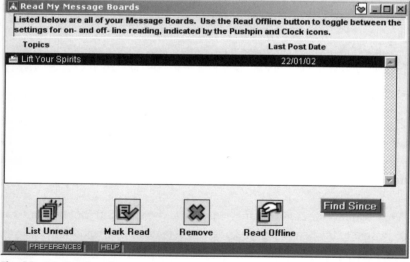

Fig. 6.8 My Boards main screen.

When you go to AOL Keyword: **My Boards**, you'll see a screen like this one, listing the topics that you've subscribed to, so you can reach all your messages with just a couple of clicks, even if they're in different parts of AOL.

List Unread and **Mark Read** work just the same way as usual, while **Remove** will remove a board from your My Boards listing.

It's all very simple – just a way of gathering everything together in one place. However, there is one important extra feature you can use from the My Boards screen.

Reading messages offline

Read Offline allows you to tell AOL that you want to collect all the messages in a particular topic when you run Automatic AOL. They'll be downloaded in one go, so you can read them at your leisure without having to stay connected all the time.

You can reply to messages offline as well, and your responses will be sent again when you next run Automatic AOL. Just click **Read Offline** after highlighting the topic you're interested in, and click it again if you decide you don't want to download the messages.

All the messages that you read offline will be stored in your Personal Filing Cabinet. You can still read messages online too, but any that you mark as read online won't be transferred to your computer when you collect new messages and email with Automatic AOL.

When you've subscribed to some message boards and marked them for reading offline, then you'll need to configure Automatic AOL. You can click **Setup Automatic AOL** on the **Email** menu, or click **Auto AOL** on your Personal Filing Cabinet.

Make sure that you check the boxes for **Send postings** and **Get unread postings** if you want to use message boards when you're not connected to AOL.

To access the messages that have been transferred to your computer, open your Personal Filing Cabinet and click on the tab labelled **Newsgroups**. You'll see a display that looks a little like that in Fig. 6.9.

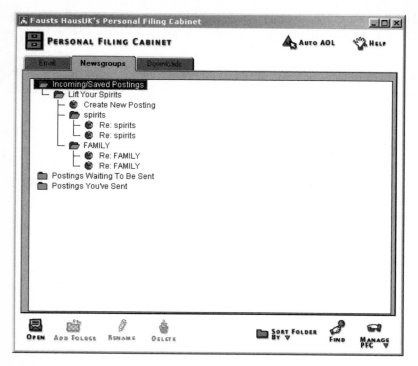

Fig. 6.9   The Newsgroups tab in your PFC.

Inside the Incoming/Saved Postings folder, you'll see folders for each of the message boards that you're subscribed to – just double-click to open one.

The folders themselves can contain more folders for each of the subjects, and there's a special entry at the top of the list for each one, labelled Create New Posting.

So, if you want to post a message to a message board when you're not connected to AOL, you need to subscribe to it, and collect messages with Automatic AOL.

Then you can go to your PFC, click the **Newsgroups** tab and move through the folders to find the appropriate one for the message board and topic that you're interested in, and click **Create New Posting**.

Fig. 6.10 Writing a message offline.

You'll see the Post New Message screen appear, and you can just type your message in, then click **Send Later**, and it will be uploaded to AOL the next time you run Automatic AOL.

When you're reading messages, they'll pop up in a screen that looks very similar to the one you read messages on when you're connected to AOL.

As you can see, there are the same buttons (though labelled slightly differently) for moving through the messages and threads. **Delete** removes the message from your computer, though not from AOL.

Instead of the single **Reply** button you'll see when you're reading messages while connected to AOL, here there are two – one to reply to the author, which sends your response via email, and one to reply to the group, which posts your comment on the message board.

And, of course, **New Message** lets you create a new posting to upload to your computer later.

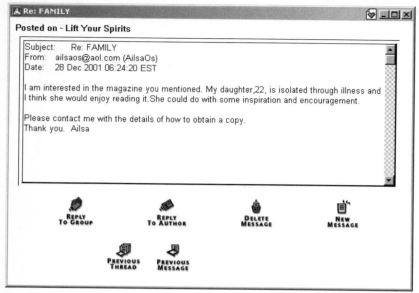

Fig. 6.11   Reading message boards offline.

If you change your mind about something you've written, you'll find it in the **Postings waiting to be sent** *section of your PFC, so you can edit or even delete it.*

That, in a nutshell, is everything you need to know about message boards. As you can see, they're pretty simple to use, and if you subscribe to boards to read offline, you can keep on top of lots of discussions without having to worry about tying up your phone line.

Now you know all about message boards, Instant Message, chat, and email. But there's still one great feature that AOL provides to help you bring people together and make your own online communities. In the next chapter, you can find out all about Groups@AOL.

7

Groups and Web Sites

Groups@AOL

So far, we've looked at four different ways of communicating with other people – email, Instant Message, chat rooms, and message boards. Wouldn't it be great if there was a way of bringing everything together, so you could build your own virtual community?

Well, that's what Groups@AOL is all about. Whatever you do in your life, chances are you do many things in groups of people – it might be colleagues, or family members, or people who attend the same night school as you.

Whatever the occasion, you can probably think of times when you might need to get some information to everyone, or when it would be useful to have everyone in one place. For example, you might need to tell all the people in your amateur dramatic group that the church hall isn't available for this week's rehearsal.

Or maybe you want to break the news that you're leaving your job to a few selected colleagues before everyone else knows.

You might want to arrange an online chat with all the members of your family to break the news that you're getting married, or maybe you'd like to show them all the picture of the house that you plan to buy for holidays in the south of France.

Groups@AOL can do all of this – and plenty more, too. You can join or create lots of different Groups, so you could be a member of one for your family, another for the local drama society, another for the friends you practise speaking French with, and so on.

*You can also invite people who aren't AOL members to join your Group – all they have to do is register for a Screen Name and they'll be able to take part, along with you and your AOL-using friends. Once you've set up your Group, show your friends the instructions for getting their own Screen Name in **Chapter 9, AOL Anywhere**.*

9 AIM

And regardless of whether the people you invite to join your Group are AOL members, or connected to the Internet in a different way, you can be sure that it's only those people who can see what your Group is about. So if you've set up a Group to help plan a surprise party, you don't need to worry about anyone else finding out. If you haven't invited someone to join, AOL won't let them see what you're up to!

Setting up a new Group

Groups

To access Groups@AOL, type AOL Keyword: **Groups**. If you've not visited it before, you'll see a welcoming screen telling you more about Groups, with a large button to create a new Group, and a link that will tell you more.

It's surprisingly easy to get started with a Group. Just think of a name – it can't contain spaces, and should be between four and sixteen letters long – and type it into the first Group Setup screen, which appears when you click **Create a Group**.

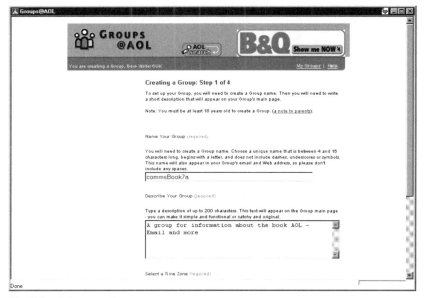

Fig. 7.1   Giving your Group a name.

The name you give your Group will be part of its Web address, so to make it easy for people to access, you should try to use as short a name as you can, provided you can make it meaningful. AOL will tell you if the name you've chosen isn't suitable, for example if it's too long.

You'll also need to give a description of your Group, to tell visitors what the Group is all about, so make sure it's full of useful information.

Next, scroll down and say what time zone you're in, then read the Groups@AOL Guidelines, and click the box next to **I Agree**, and then click **Submit Information**.

Now you're well on your way to having a Group set up. On the next page, you can choose a theme for your Group, which is a sort of template, which decides the order that some of the options on your Group pages will appear in. You can choose from Family, Friends, and Activity.

You can also type in a short title, which will appear on the top of all the pages, so if you called your Group SmithFamily you might give a title of The Smith Family Group.

When you've made your choices, click **Submit Information**, and go on to the next page, where you can choose a style. That will control the colours, icons and so on that make up the look of your pages. You can pick from the examples and, once again, click **Submit** to move on to the next stage.

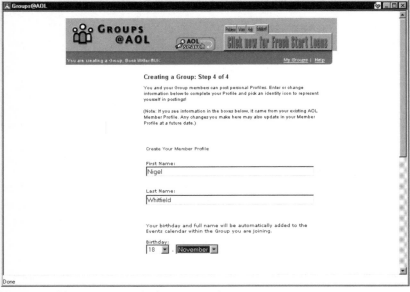

Fig. 7.2 Adding your personal information to the Group.

This is almost the last page! On this screen, you need to enter your name and a profile, which will tell other people a little bit about you. That way, when people receive your invitation to join the Group, if they don't know you already, they'll be able to find out a little more about the person who's managing it.

You have to enter your first and last names, at the very least. And you can also choose an icon to represent you in the Group – just click next to the one that you think is most appropriate to your personality.

Finally, click **Submit Information**, and you'll see a screen confirming that your Group has been set up, and giving some extra information.

For example, you'll see that there's a Group Web Address, which would be something like http://groups.aol.co.uk/fredandwilma. That's the address that people on the Internet can type into their Web browser to visit your Group.

You'll also receive an email from AOL with all the details in it. You should keep it in a safe place and make sure you read the extra information it contains about Groups.

As the creator of a Group, you have extra responsibilities to make sure all the members behave. Remember to read the information you're sent carefully.

There are two links on the page. One, **Visit Your New Group**, will take you to a page where you can see results of your efforts, while the other is labelled **Invite Some Members**.

Inviting members to your Group

Like a club, a Group isn't much use if there aren't any other members! The invitation page lets you invite up to ten people at a time to join your Group, and the invites you send out will be valid for four weeks – if someone hasn't replied by then, you'll have to re-invite them.

On this screen, you can type the addresses of the people you want to invite into the boxes at the top, and then a personalised message at the bottom.

You might say, for example 'I thought this would be a good idea for planning our holiday – and we can upload pictures when we get back.' If you don't type a message, they'll just see the standard invitation, which you can read at the bottom of the screen.

Fig. 7.3   Inviting people to join your new Group.

Click **Send Invitations** when you've added the addresses of all the people you want to be in your Group, and then sit back and wait for them to join.

If the people you're inviting are AOL members or already have a Screen Name to use with AIM, you can just type their Screen Name. But for people who don't have a Screen Name yet, you need to enter their full email address.

When you visit your Group, you'll see that you're listed as the founder, which gives you special rights, such as the ability to invite other people, or to delete the Group. We'll explain more about managing your Group later on in this chapter.

When you've been invited to a Group

Everyone who's invited to join a Group receives an email message, which contains a standard invitation plus any special message typed by the Group's founder when they sent the invitation.

All you need to do is click on the link that's included in the message, and then follow the instructions on the Web page that will open on your computer.

If you're an AOL member, or you've already signed up for AOL Instant Messenger, you can use an existing Screen Name and password to access the Group you've been invited to join. If you don't already have a Screen Name, just follow the instructions to create one.

You can read more about Screen Names, and using them with the AOL Instant Messenger™ service, in **Chapter 9, AOL Anywhere***.*

9 AIM

Once you sign in to Groups@AOL with a Screen Name and password, you'll have to fill in a member profile form, giving your first and last names, and a little bit of information about yourself, which other Group members will be able to read. Choose an icon to represent yourself in the Group, then read the guidelines and confirm that you agree with them.

An important word on Group invitations

Groups are a great way to get people together and to share information, but what happens in a Group is controlled solely by the founder and the other members. While there are guidelines that everyone has to agree to, some parents might feel that certain Groups aren't appropriate for their children.

To help make sure your child is safe online, if a Screen Name that's marked as Teens or Kids Only via AOL's Parental Controls is invited to a Group, the master Screen Name for that account will also be automatically invited to join the same Group – a bit like having your parent take you along to a party.

When the Master Screen Name associated with a particular child leaves a Group, the child will also be removed from the membership list – in other words, a child can't be a member of a Group unless the person responsible for their Screen Name is also a member.

Using Groups@AOL

Creating a Group is simple, but now you need to make the most of it. Thankfully, that's really simple too. Let's start with how you access the Group.

> Groups

If you're using the AOL software on your computer, just go to AOL Keyword: **Groups**, and you'll see a list of all the Groups you're a member of. Click the name of the Group that you want to visit.

Wherever you are, using the AOL software or not, you can also connect to your Groups via the **groups.aol.co.uk** Web page – just type the address into the **Keyword** bar in AOL or the address bar of any Web browser, and click the **sign-in** link if you're not connected via AOL.

You can also go directly to the page for a particular Group, by putting the Group name on the end of the address, preceded by a "/", for example **groups.aol.co.uk/tg6group**.

Finding your way around a Group page is pretty easy; as you can see there are a few sections listed down the left hand side, and a main area of the screen with the latest information in some of the sections.

The order of all the sections will depend on the theme that you chose, and there are different styles for Group pages too, so the ones that you join won't look exactly like the pictures here, though they'll work in the same way.

Down the left, you'll see options for the Main page, which is the first one you see when you visit a Group. Other options are See Photos, View Events, Browse Favourites, Read Postings, Send Group Email, View Members and Edit your profile.

Underneath those main options, there's a button that says **Enter Group Chat**. When you click on it, you'll be taken to a chat room just for your Group, where you can talk with other members.

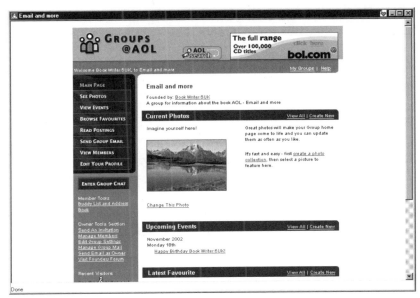

Fig. 7.4 The main page of your new Group.

If you want to take part in Group chats when you're accessing your Group pages without using the AOL software, you need to download the latest version of AOL Instant Messenger (AIM) to use Group Chat.

Look a little lower, and you'll see a link that says **Buddy List**, which you can use to automatically add all the members of the Group to your Buddy List™ with just a couple of clicks, instead of having to type them all in manually.

There's also a list of recent visitors, and you'll see a little icon of a walking man next to the name of any Group members who are still signed on and available for you to reach via an Instant Message.

If you're the founder or owner of a Group, you'll also see a set of links labelled **Owner Tools**. *You can read about them later in this chapter.*

As you scroll down the main page, you'll see that the title bar for each section has two links on the right; one is labelled **View All**, and the other **Create New**. Clicking on **View All** will take you to a page where you can see all the information in that section of the Group pages – just like clicking the big buttons down the left of the screen. **Create New** lets you make a new entry.

So, that's the main screen, but what are all the different things that Groups offer you?

Photos

Group photos lets you upload your own photographs to the AOL computers, so that other members of the Group can browse through them. You can upload pictures in collections, a bit like an electronic version of a photo album.

If you do that, it makes it easier for other people to browse through the pictures, without having to see the ones they're not interested in. You can also choose a picture to be featured on the main page.

Events

The Events section is where you can add details of things like group outings, or birthdays, so that everyone who joins your Group can see them when they view the page.

You might, for example, add the date of your club's AGM, or the annual dinner-dance for the colleagues at work. You can even add an anniversary, so that you don't forget – or so that all the members of your Group know how long it is before they need to think about all the presents for your silver wedding.

Normally, the Events section of the Group pages just shows what's happening in the current month, but you can browse through other months to check what's coming up as well.

Favourites

Group Favourites is a place where members can add links to their favourite sites, or write a short comment about a new book or film they've seen. You could even type a short recipe for everyone to look at, and you can rate all the favourites you add by awarding them up to five stars.

If you're thinking of organising a group outing, for example, you could encourage everyone to describe their favourite restaurant, then all the members could read the comments and decide where they want to go.

Postings

Postings in a Group are like a sticky note stuck to the Group page; you could use them for a discussion, or for an important piece of news that you want everyone to see when they check the Group pages – like a change of venue for a party, perhaps.

If you want to be absolutely sure that everyone sees a posting, you can even have it automatically sent to all the members via email, so it's great for last minute announcements that simply have to get to everyone. They'll know what's happened, even if they don't sign on to the Group page.

Group email

Group email is one of the most useful ways of keeping in touch, or carrying on a discussion, when the members of your Group can't all be available at the same time to send Instant Messages or have a Group chat.

With Group email, you just have to remember one email address, and you can send a message to all the members. In fact, you don't even have to remember that – you can fill in a form on the Group email page, and AOL will do the work for you!

If you're away from your computer, and you just want to send a quick message to everyone, it's easy – just use the address groupname@groups.aol.com. For example, if you have a Group called tg6group, then just send an email message to tg6group@groups.aol.com.

It really is simple, isn't it? You can send a message to the founder and owners of the Group too; the details of the addresses to use are on the Group email page.

View Members

The View Members section shows you a list of all the different members in the Group, along with their full name. You'll see the icon that they chose to represent them, and you can view their profile by clicking their name. If you click their email address instead, you'll be able to send them a message.

Your Profile

The Profile button lets you change the description of yourself on the Group pages, so if you've graduated from university, perhaps you'd like to tell people here and be subtle, rather than make a special posting and have people think you're boasting!

Adding information to the Group pages

Using Groups@AOL is very simple. When you click to create a new entry in any of the sections, you'll see a simple form that you have to fill in, giving the details of the event, favourite, posting, or whatever you want to add.

Just follow the instructions on the screen, and in no time at all, you'll be sharing information with all the other members of the Group.

Let's have a look at adding photographs to your Group page in more detail – once you've done that, you'll have no problems sharing any other type of information with your fellow members.

The first step in adding pictures to your Group page is giving your collection of pictures a name, which you should make as descriptive as possible. People who visit the Group pages will see the name you type in, and your screen name, so they know who created each collection.

After you've filled in the screen asking you for a name, you'll see a new page like the one in Fig. 7.5 appear.

All you have to do is click **Browse** and choose one of the pictures that you have on your computer's hard disk. If you've already put a picture on a Web site, you can just give the address of the picture instead, which will save you having to upload it.

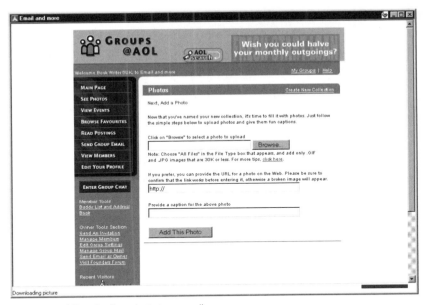

Fig. 7.5   Adding the first photo to your album.

Finally, add a caption for the photograph, and click **Add This Photo**. Once your picture has been transferred to the AOL computers, you'll be asked if you want to add more pictures, or you can just click **I've Finished**, and you'll be asked if you want to feature one of your new photographs on the main page, where everyone will see it as soon as they sign on.

Adding photos is the most complicated part of using Groups@AOL. If you've managed that, you should be all set to use all the other features without any problems at all – but if you do get stuck, you can always click **Help** at the top right of each page.

Now you know how to add information to the pages, and how you can chat with other members, or send them messages to tell them the latest news, you'll be able to make the most of Groups, whether it's for work or pleasure. In fact, before long, you'll probably wonder how you managed without them.

Managing your Group

If you created a Group, you're known as the founder, and as we explained earlier, that means it's up to you to make sure everything runs smoothly.

When you visit a Group that you founded, you'll see a set of extra links on the left hand side of the page, above the Recent Visitors, that are labelled **Owner Tools**.

What's an owner? Well, the founder is the person in complete control of a Group, but if you want other people to be able to invite new members to join, or remove anyone who breaks the rules, then you can make them an owner, so that they can help in the administration.

So if you've set up a Group for a club, for example, you might decide to add the club secretary and treasurer as owners, so that they help manage things online as well as in real life.

There are five extra links that Group founders and owners will see: Send An Invitation, Manage Members, Edit Group Settings, Manage Group Email and Send Email as Owner.

Send An Invitation takes you to the same screen we showed earlier, where you can type in the Screen Names or email addresses of people you want to invite to your Group.

If you want to share the workload with someone else by making them an owner, **Manage Members** is the link you need. When you click it, you'll see a screen like that in Fig. 7.6.

As you can see, there's a list of all the members, together with their full name, the icon they chose, and a Status entry, which tells you if they're an ordinary member, an owner, or the founder.

Click on the Screen Name to read a member's profile. The really useful links here, though, are the ones labelled **Edit** and **Delete**.

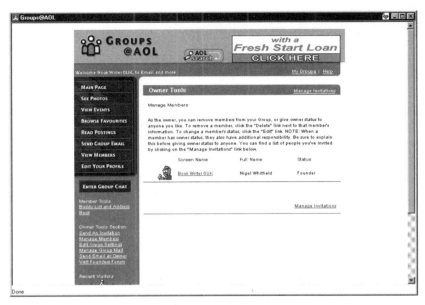

Fig. 7.6 Managing the members of your Group.

Delete is used to remove someone from your Group – perhaps someone's been posting inappropriate comments to the Group mailing list, or they misbehaved at the last meeting you had. When you click **Delete**, you'll be given the choice of sending out a standard letter telling someone they've been removed, or typing your own explanation. You could, for example, tell someone which of your club rules they've breached.

> *If you remove a Screen Name from your Group that is the Screen Name of the parent of another member with either Teen or Kids Only Parental Controls settings, their child's membership will be revoked as well.*

On the Edit screen, you can change someone's status to make them an owner, so that they can help you out – owners can invite other people to join, or remove people from the Group.

At the top of the Manage Members screen, there's one other option – a link labelled **Manage Invitations**. You can click on it to review the invitations you've sent and see who has yet to respond – and if, for example, someone's moved away or changed jobs, you can click to delete their invitation so that even if they do reply, they won't be able to join your Group any more.

The **Edit Group Settings** page allows you to change the title on your main page, and the description, so you might perhaps change the title to reflect the play you're planning to put on in the school hall this year, and give an appropriate description – it's simpler than having to create a new Group, as long as you're happy with the name you already have.

The other option on the **Edit Group Settings** page lets you delete your Group completely. You can either have a standard message sent to all the members, or type your own. You might, for example, want to delete a Group if you created it just for planning a special event which has now passed.

When you delete a Group, that's it! You can't get it back, and all the pictures and other information people added to the pages are gone forever. So don't click **Delete** unless you mean it.

The **Manage Group Email** screen will tell you if there is a problem with the email addresses for any of the Group members. Hopefully, you'll hardly ever need to use it, but sometimes, for a variety of reasons, it's not possible to send email to people.

It's a good idea to check this page from time to time and see if there are any problems – especially if someone tells you they've not received any emails from the Group.

If there are problems with sending mail, then AOL will automatically stop sending messages to someone in your Group; you can use the page to start sending messages again, or to delete someone from your Group if you think that they won't be able to access it again.

The final option in the Owner Tools section, **Send Email as Owner**, is the one to use when you want to add a stamp of authority to your message. Normally, if you send an email to the Group email address, it will have your usual name on it. That might be OK if you're just having a conversation with people.

But sometimes, you might need to remind people who's in charge – perhaps to defuse an argument, or just as a regular message to tell people about how your Group or club is run.

Fig. 7.7   Sending an email as the Group owner.

When you use the **Send Email as Owner** option, instead of writing your email in the usual way, you just fill in a form on the screen and click **Send**. Instead of having your own email address, it will have a special one – for example, if your Group is called tg6group, then the email will appear to come from tg6group-owner@groups.aol.com.

And that's just about all you need to know about Groups! As you can see, they're very easy to set up, and to participate in. You don't need to know anything complicated, and even if you're the founder or owner, there's plenty of help to keep things running smoothly.

So, whether it's a community group planning a street party, a set of colleagues working on a new project, or a way of keeping in touch with all the members of your family, around the world, set up a Group today, and start sharing online.

Web sites

Groups@AOL is a superb way of keeping a select number of people informed, but as we've stressed already, your Group pages are private – they can only be seen by people that have been invited to join.

Wouldn't it be great if there was an easy way to put information on the Web so that anyone could access it?

You could, for example, make a Web page to tell people all about your hobbies and interests, in considerably more detail than an AOL Member Profile allows. Or you could put pictures of yourself on there, so people you chat to can see them easily.

You might be a painter, and want to show people examples of your work, or a collector of classic cars who wants to show off your latest purchase.

Whatever the reason, building a Web page is a great way to let people know who you are and what you're interested in. And if you put together a good page, you'll often find that people will contact you after reading it, giving you another way to make new friends online.

Hometown

When you signed up for AOL, you were automatically given space to make your own Web pages in the Hometown area, with 20Mb of space for each of your screen names. And you don't need to know anything about Web page building – AOL provides you with tools so simple that anyone can have a home page in minutes.

Once you've created Web pages, anyone on the Internet will be able to visit them – they don't need to be an AOL member, or sign up for a Screen Name. All you need to do is tell people your Web address, and they can read everything that you've decided to put on your pages. People with similar interests will also be able to find your pages using Hometown's search facility.

Your Screen Name, as well as being your email address, is part of your Web address. So if your Screen Name is BookWriter6uk, for example, your Web address will start like this: http://hometown.aol.co.uk/ BookWriter6uk.

To make it easy to find people with similar interests, your Web pages in AOL Hometown are put in one of the 'communities', which group Web sites together. That way, when you browse through the pages, you can quickly find more people that you might have something in common with, whether it's a love of a particular film star or of fine food.

Getting started in AOL Hometown
It's easy to start building your own Web site: all you need to do is go to AOL Keyword: **Hometown** and you'll see a screen like this one appear, which offers you a number of ways to create and change your Web pages.

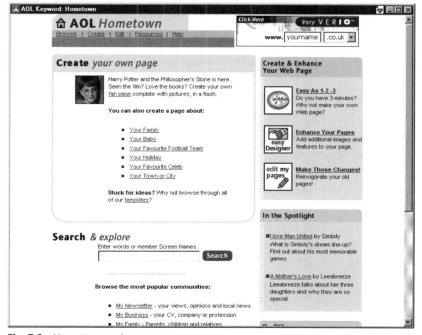

Fig. 7.8 Hometown main screen.

If you're not sure what you want to make a page about, why not start your visit to AOL Hometown by browsing through the pages that other members have created. Just follow the links from the Hometown front page.

We're going to start here by looking at how you can create a page using AOL's 1-2-3 Publish system, which is designed to help you create your first Web pages with hardly any work at all.

Once you've got the hang of that, or if you just want to jump in at the deep end, we'll look at Easy Designer, which will let you change pages you've already created, or start a new one from scratch. What's the difference between the two? Well, Easy Designer will let you use your own creative ideas much more easily, but if you've never made a Web page before, it might seem a little too complicated.

1-2-3 Publish

1-2-3 Publish

Building your first Web page is really simple. To get started, you need to click **1-2-3 Publish** on the AOL Keyword: **Hometown** page.

The first step is choosing a theme for your page. On the first page of 1-2-3 Publish, you can pick from a range of templates covering a wide range of categories. Click on one of the categories – here we've chosen a template for a Web page about pets.

On the next screen, you can choose options like a background colour for your page, and type in a title. You can also select a picture for the top of your page from a selection – just click the box next to each of the options that you want to select. You can even choose a picture from your computer's hard disk – just click **Browse** to select one.

When you've done that, scroll down the page and you'll see more options, including boxes where you can type the text that you'd like to appear on the page, for example an amusing story about your pet.

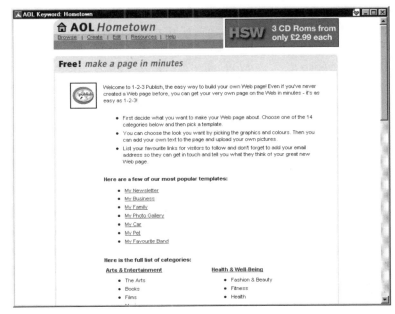

Fig. 7.9 1-2-3 Publish main screen.

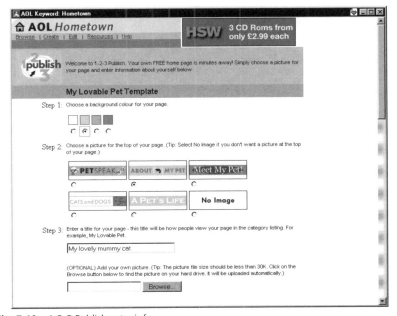

Fig. 7.10 1-2-3 Publish extra info.

Just type the information that you want in each box, and select which type of divider you'd like to appear between each of the sections.

You don't have to fill in information for all the different boxes, but if you leave them blank, AOL will still put the dividers in between each of the sections of the page.

After you've filled in all the information you want, scroll down again, and you'll see some more boxes where you can enter links to Web sites that you think visitors to your page might be interested in.

Below those are two more buttons, **Save My Page** and **Preview My Page**. If you click the first one, you'll see what your page will look like, and it'll be made available to everyone on the Web. Click **Preview My Page** instead, and you'll be able to see what the end result is like, without everyone else being able to view it – so you can make sure you like the results, or change some of the options if you think it will make the page look better.

Fig. 7.11 1-2-3 Publish page preview.

When you preview the page, you'll see something like Fig. 7.11 – just choose **Modify** if you want to return to the previous screen to make changes, or click **Save** to allow everyone to read about your pet.

When your page has been saved, you'll see a screen like the one below, telling you the Web address where people can find it, and you'll also receive an email with the same information, just to make sure you don't forget.

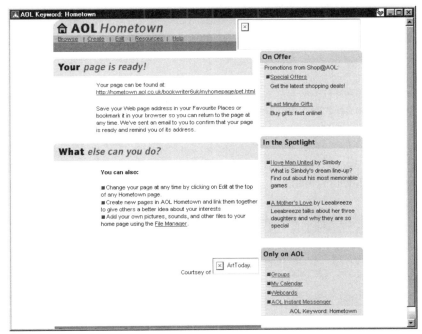

Fig. 7.12 1-2-3 Publish – page saved.

And that really is all there is to making your own page! If you'd like to do something a little more unique, or if you want to change a page you've already made, then you can be more creative with AOL's Easy Designer.

Easy Designer

Easy Designer

So, now you've created a page with 1-2-3 Publish and you want to make it a little more unique. Or perhaps you already know a little about Web pages, and want to do something more complicated than 1-2-3 Publish allows. Either way, just click **Easy Designer** on the main Hometown page to get started.

When Easy Designer starts, you'll be asked if you want to create a new page, or change an existing one. If you've already made a Web page, you can change it, but for now we'll just see how to make a new one, so click on the text **Create a new page**. Changing a page you've already made, for example with 1-2-3 Publish, is almost the same – except that the page you've already made will appear, so you don't have to choose from the different categories.

Easy Designer can take a little while to start running, especially if you have an old computer. Just be patient and wait until the message "Easy Designer is Ready" appears on the screen.

The first stage of building a page is selecting a category for it, from the list that appears on your screen.

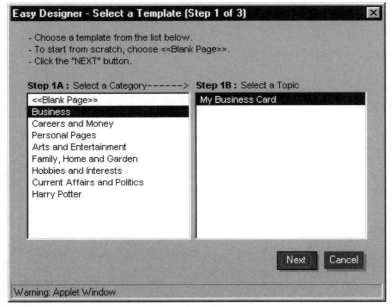

Fig. 7.13   Easy Designer category list.

You can start with a completely blank page, but it's best to use one of the templates. The category you choose will help people find your page when they're browsing through AOL Hometown. Just click the category and topic that you want to use, then click **Next**.

Now you'll see some sample layouts, showing where pictures, headlines and text will appear on your page. Pick the layout that's closest to what you want – you can change everything around later if you like. When you've made your choice, click **Next** again.

After choosing the layout, you'll be asked to pick a colour scheme. Just click on the name of the scheme on the left, and you'll see on the right how it will affect the text on your page. When you've made your choice, click **OK** and Easy Designer will set up a basic page based on the choices that you've just made. Click **Let's Go** to start adding your own information to the page.

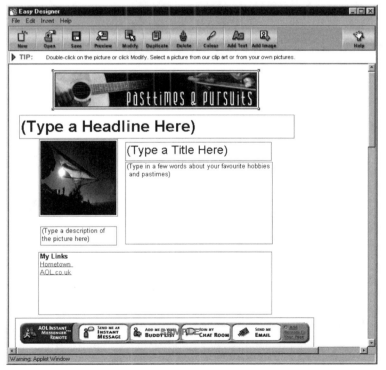

Fig. 7.14   Easy Designer main screen.

When the basic page has been set up, you'll see a screen like the one in Fig. 7.14, with short headings in all the boxes for text, and dummy pictures. If you want to move something around on the page, all you have to do is click on it with your mouse, then hold the mouse button down as you drag it to the new location.

To make sure that you don't accidentally leave things on top of each other, Easy Designer will let you know when two of the items on your page are overlapping. Just carry on moving one of them and the message will disappear.

If you want to change the text in one of the boxes, all you need to do is double-click the box. After a brief pause, you'll see a new window appear on the screen, where you can type in the text that you want to go in the box.

Fig. 7.15 Easy Designer text edit box.

Just type the information that you want to appear on your Web page. If you've already got something written, for example a poem in a word processor, you can copy the information from that program by highlighting it with the mouse and pressing Ctrl-C, then clicking Easy Designer's text box and pressing Ctrl-V to paste the text in.

You can also use the buttons along the top of the box to change the size, colour or style of the text, just as if you were using a word processor.

Making a link

You can even make some of the text in your box link to another page, either on your own AOL Hometown pages, or anywhere else on the Internet.

To make a link, highlight the text that you want to use – perhaps the phrase "Click here" – and then click **Link This Text**.

Fig. 7.16   Easy Designer lnk box.

You have a choice of three different types of link that you can make on this screen. Just click next to the appropriate one.

If you're making a link to somewhere else on the Internet, choose the first option, and then type the full Internet address, for example http://www.bbc.co.uk/, into the box.

To make a link to one of your own Hometown pages, choose the second option, and then pick one of your pages from the list by clicking the arrow to the right of the box – so you don't need to worry about mistyping the name of a page you've already created. Of course, if you haven't made any other pages yet, there won't be any to choose from in the box.

Finally, if you want to make a link to an email address, choose the third option and type an email address into the box. When you do this, people can click on the link and their email program will automatically start, ready to send a new message to the address you gave.

Pictures on your Web page

If you'd like to change the pictures on your page, just double-click on one of the pictures, and the Easy Designer Picture Gallery will start. It looks something like this.

Fig. 7.17   Easy Designer Picture Gallery.

You can choose from AOL's selection of pictures on the left, and move around the different categories of picture by clicking on the text above the picture. **Link This Object** allows you to make a picture into a button that people can click on, and works just like linking text. But what about using a picture of your own? No problem.

If you'd like to add one of your own pictures, whether or yourself, your home or your pet cat, all you need to do is click **Upload Picture**.

Fig. 7.18   Easy Designer Upload Picture screen.

Click **Browse**, and locate the picture on your computer's hard disk drive, then click **Upload Picture** to send your picture to AOL, and it'll be automatically added to the gallery, so you can select it to use on your Web page.

You only need to upload a picture once, even if you use it on all your Web pages. Once the picture has been uploaded, you can find it in the Picture Gallery by looking for the category called My Pictures, which appears at the top of the list.

Remember that large pictures will take longer to download, making your site seem slow to visitors. You should try to use pictures saved in the JPEG (or .jpg) format, and don't make them any larger than necessary.

Editing your page

If you decide that you want more pictures on your page, or more boxes of text, all you need to do is click the buttons at the top of the Easy Designer window, labelled **Add Text** or **Add Image**. Similarly, if you want to delete a picture or a section of text from your page, just click to highlight it, and then use the **Delete** button at the top of the Easy Designer window.

Colour allows you to alter the colour scheme of your page, if you decide that it doesn't look very nice in the one that you chose originally.

Click **Duplicate** if you want to make a copy of something already on your page. For example, you might have a picture that you put at the top of your page that takes you to a favourite site, and want it at the bottom too. Just click to highlight it, then press **Duplicate**, and a new copy will appear, which you can drag to wherever you want on the page.

Modify brings up the same screen you'll see when you double click on one of the items on your page – so if you click it when you've highlighted a picture, you'll see the picture gallery, for example.

Checking and saving your page

When you've finished adding information to your page, you'll want to see what it looks like before it goes live. Click **Preview** to see how the results will look when you save your page.

You'll see the preview appear in a new window on your computer screen, just like the picture in Fig. 7.19. You should see the **Easy Designer** icon appear in the Task Bar at the bottom of your screen; click it when you've finished looking at the preview, and either make changes to the page, or click **Save** at the top of the window.

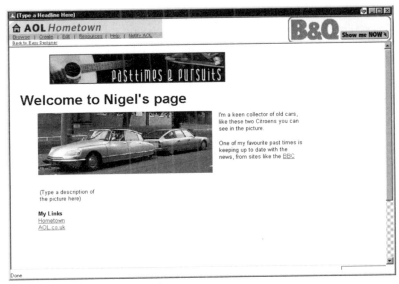

Fig. 7.19 Easy Designer page preview.

When you choose to save your page, you'll see the screen below. Type a title for the page in the first box, and then a filename in the second one.

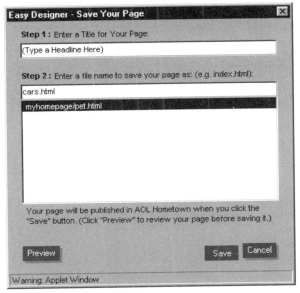

Fig. 7.20 Easy Designer save screen.

The filename should end in .html, and in the box below, you'll see a list of the pages you've already created, so you can make sure you don't pick a name that's already taken. People can go directly to the page by putting its name on the end of your hometown address. So, if your screen name is BookWriter6uk, and you call a page aboutme.html, people can go directly to it with the Web address http://hometown.aol.co.uk/bookwriter6uk/aboutme.html

The name index.html is a special one – it's reserved for the first page of your Web site. When you call a file index.html, people don't need to put it on the end of your Web address. Instead, it will appear automatically when people visit your Web address, for example http://hometown.aol.co.uk/bookwriter6uk/

After your page has been saved, you'll automatically see it appear in the AOL browser, so you can be sure of how it looks. You can use **New** in Easy Designer to start another page, or click **Open** if you'd like to make changes to a page that you saved previously.

And that's all there is to it – you really can have a Web site with pictures, links, and lots of information to tell people all about you and your hobbies in just a few minutes. After you have saved a page for the first time using 1-2-3 Publish or Easy Designer, you will see a confirmation page and Hometown will also send you a confirmation email. Both of these contain the address of your Web page so that you can send it to your friends and family.

CHAPTER

8

Help and Advice on AOL

Now we've looked at all the different ways you can communicate on AOL, and along the way we've come up with plenty of suggestions for how you can use the different tools, like email, the AOL Instant Messenger™ service, message boards, and so on.

In this chapter, we're going to highlight some of the different types of help and advice available on AOL, from some of the specialised chat rooms and message boards, to the online guides that you'll find in every one of AOL's channels.

What sort of things can you expect to find? Well, just about anything, to be frank. The help and advice areas on AOL cover topics ranging from health and fitness to homework, from computing to agony aunts (and uncles!).

There are so many different areas where you can seek help and advice that we've grouped them together into broad topics, so you can find the information you want quickly. And don't forget that you can reach any of the areas here by pressing Ctrl-K (Apple-K on a Mac) and typing in the AOL Keyword for the area.

AOL's message boards and chat rooms are usually open all the time, but some of the Hosted chats have a timetable, so check online to see the details. Hosted chats are ones where someone from AOL, like a technical expert or an agony uncle, will be online and in the chat room, ready to speak with people. Some of the chat rooms will stay open when the Host has left, others won't – but you'll always find all the details at the AOL Keywords we give.

Quick Chat

Don't forget, too, that you can always find someone to chat with, just by going to AOL Keyword: **Quick Chat** and scrolling through the list of chat rooms until you find one that looks interesting to you. You can also click **Chat and Communities** on the channel bar, and pick a chat area from there, or choose one of the message boards to post your comments to.

In this chapter, we'll be looking at some of the ways you can get the help and advice that you're looking for. Broadly speaking, there are two types of advice – there's the informal advice that you can find from other AOL members, and then there's the specialised information and advice that you can receive from people who are on AOL just to help you out, whether it's an emotional problem, health, or something wrong with your PC. AOL has experts in lots of areas to provide you with the information you need, or point you to the solution to your problems.

So, let's start by looking at the specialists you can find on AOL, before we take a look at some of the best places to find informal tips and advice from other users.

Specialist help and advice

AOL has experts covering all sorts of areas, from help with your computer to emotional problems. Here are some of the most useful ones.

AOL help

As you'd expect from an online service like AOL, there are plenty of places where you can get help and advice about all sort of aspects of computing. As well as the online help with things like account details and using email that you'll find at AOL Keyword: **Help**, there's also the AOL Keyword: **Tech Chat** area where you can speak directly with one of AOL's support team, if you have any problems.

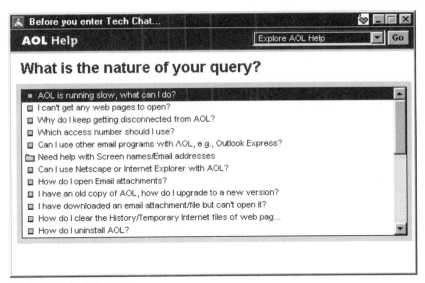

Fig. 8.1   Tech Chat screen.

When you visit Tech Chat, you can talk one-to-one with someone from the AOL support team, so you don't have to disconnect from AOL and pick up the phone to solve your problem.

Finance

Ask The Experts

Financial matters can be bewildering at the best of times, but getting it right is important and can save you money, whether it's the best type of mortgage, or how to fill in your Self Assessment form.

At AOL Keyword: **Ask The Experts**, you can pose your questions about financial matters and be sure that they'll be answered by leading experts in the field. Do you want to know if there are pitfalls in cashing in an endowment policy early? Or how you can check up on your credit rating? Then this is the place to look. If your question isn't one of the ones picked for an answer, take a look at the archive of previous questions.

Remember that although AOL has experts online to answer your financial questions, you should always remember that advice given will depend on the information you supply. You should always seek detailed financial advice from a suitably qualified professional advisor before making any decisions.

Kids and teenagers

Ask A Teacher

Dear Joanie

Stressed Out

AOL has plenty of specialist advice for kids, both young and old.

Whether it's worries about moving to a new school, or problems at home, there's a place for children to get help. For the younger members, there's agony aunt Joanie, who solves problems each week at AOL Keyword: **Dear Joanie**. There are regular hosted chats with Joanie, too, so kids can speak to her live, instead of just sending in a message.

For slightly older kids, agony uncle Matt Whyman is on hand to dispense advice, whether it's problems with young love or exam stress. You can call for his help at AOL Keyword: **Stressed Out**.

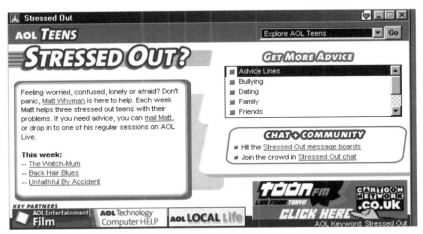

Fig. 8.2   Stressed Out.

As well as providing lots of online reference material in the Research & Learn channel, AOL has a team of teachers standing by to help out with schoolwork if you get stuck. Just send in your question at AOL Keyword: **Ask A Teacher** and they'll do their best to reply within 48 hours.

Love and relationships

Dr Pam

No matter how hard we work at them, in most relationships there are times when it's helpful to get an outside perspective. What might seem like a massive problem to you could have a surprisingly simple solution – but who should you ask?

AOL has its own agony aunt, relationships expert Dr Pam Spurr, who can provide professional advice and suggestions to help you sort things out. And if you want a broader perspective, her section of AOL has a message area too, so you can share your problems with other members, or offer your own solutions to theirs.

Travel

Travel Expert

If you're travelling around the world, and want to know about a particular country, why not ask the **Travel Expert**? At this AOL Keyword, you'll find a list of all the experts that you can contact, whatever type of holiday or trip you're planning. Fancy a safari? Or an adventure holiday? Or would you like to know about local conditions in the Caribbean?

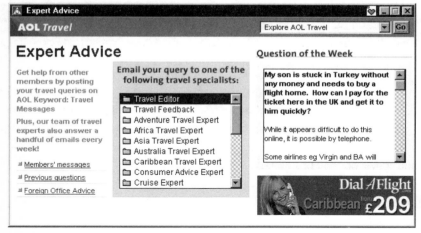

Fig. 8.3 Travel Expert.

AOL's travel editors are here to help you, and you can send your question directly to them for information or tips. You'll also be able to see the answers to questions asked by other members, covering a range of vital topics, from holiday insurance to what to pack for a cruise holiday.

Ask other members

One of the greatest resources on AOL is the community of members. As well as being a great way to make new friends, they're also an amazing resource when you have a problem. There might not be someone in your street who knows the answer to your problem – whether it's fixing a car or a PC – but there's probably someone, somewhere else in the world. And with over a million members in the UK, and 33 million around the world, AOL gives you an awful lot of brains to pick!

Here, then, are some of the best places to look on AOL for help, advice, inspiration, or just to talk over a problem with other people like you. We've grouped them into subjects, so you can find the things you want easily – just go to the AOL Keywords we've listed. And don't forget that you can find plenty more on the Chat and Communities channel, too.

Computer help

> Web Building

> Mac

> Computing Chat

One of the great things about an online service such as AOL is the huge number of people who can help you with things to do with your computer. You might find experts from software companies spending their evenings chatting, or other relative newcomers who want to share their experiences.

Perhaps you're building your first Web page, and you're not sure where to start – or maybe you want more information on how to do some of the fancier Web tricks that you've seen on other people's sites. Click on the AOL Keyword: **Web Building** section in AOL Keyword: **Computing Chat**, and you can swap tips and horror stories with other people in the chat rooms and message boards.

These chat rooms are open all the time, and you'll also find Hosted chats twice a week, where you can be sure there'll be experts on hand to answer your questions.

You'll find plenty of other computing chats, including Practical PC chat for the readers of *Practical PC* magazine, PC Music chat, Beginners Computing, Windows, Office and Anti-virus chat too. There's even a regular chat for gadgets and gizmos, so you can ask people's opinion of the latest electronic toys before you buy them. And if you're an Apple Macintosh user, there's a chat room specially for you, at AOL Keyword: **Mac**.

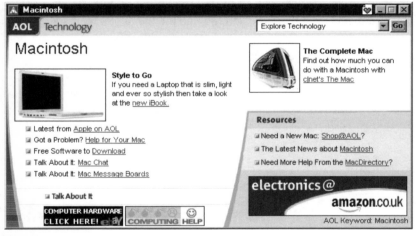

Fig. 8.4 Mac.

Health advice

Health Chat

Keeping healthy is important, and there are plenty of areas on the Health channel where you can find tips and information, or post questions about things that are worrying you. As well as Hosted chats with qualified medical professionals, you can find chat rooms and messages boards at AOL Keyword:

Health Chat, where you can get advice on a question you might be too embarrassed to tell your friends about.

If you're really shy, remember that you could always create a new Screen Name on your account, so there's no danger of any colleagues or friends realising that it's you asking about an intimate problem.

Hobbies and leisure

You'll find plenty of things to talk about on AOL for different hobby and leisure interests – far more than we could hope to include here.

> Home Chat

In the AOL Keyword: **Home Chat** area, you can swap DIY and decorating tips. And there's also gardening advice from other members and qualified Hosts. You can exchange tales of your pets, or discuss just about any interest, from sewing to the Army.

> Car Club

Or if you prefer a faster pace of life, why not visit AOL Keyword: **Car Club**, where you'll be able to join in a weekly Hosted motoring chat, or just hang out with other drivers all week. There are message boards too, so you can ask for advice on that second hand dream car, see if anyone knows a quick way to change a carburettor, or just chat about classic cars.

> Entertainment Chat

If music is more your thing, you'll find message boards for just about every type at AOL Keyword: **Entertainment Chat**. You'll also find heated debates about TV, films, books, and every other type of entertainment you can imagine.

> Book Club

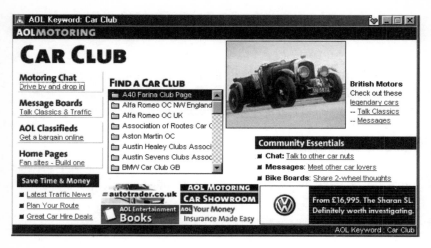

Fig. 8.5   Car Club.

Or how about wandering along to AOL Keyword: **Book Club**, hosted by award-winning novelist Mel McGrath, where you can talk with other AOL members about the latest novel you've read, or share your opinions of the book of the month.

International affairs

Travel Chat

Everyone likes to get away, whether it's for a short break or an epic journey across continents. Want to know what other people thought of a resort? Why not ask at AOL Keyword: **Travel Chat**, where you'll also find competitions and travel ideas to help you plan your holiday?

International

Bistro

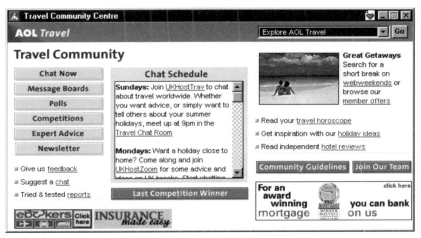

Fig. 8.6   Travel Chat.

AOL's International channel (AOL Keyword: **International**) has plenty of places to chat too; if you want talk with an international flavour, in a place where any language is welcome, visit AOL Keyword: **Bistro**. As well as the main international room, you'll see there are plenty of rooms that you can join for specific languages – so it could be a great place to brush up on your skills before leaving home.

Kids and teenagers

Teen Chat

Stressed Out

Sugar

AOL provides plenty of message boards and chat areas for your children. Though the message boards in the Kids channel are open round the clock, chat rooms are only open at certain times – and when they are, they're all looked after by a trained Host.

*Don't forget that you can use AOL's Parental Controls, described in **Chapter 10, Online Guidelines**. If you set your child's access to Kids Only – recommended for under-12s – your child will only be able to access the Hosted chats in the Kids channel.*

10 It's all in the name

Teenagers love to chat, and at AOL Keyword: **Teen Chat** you'll find some of the liveliest message boards, including AOL Keyword: **Stressed Out**, for problem sharing, and AOL Keyword: **Sugar**, for girls to gossip about everything from boys to make-up.

Local life

LL Chat

If you want to know the answer to a question, ask a local. And the Local Life channel is where you can find all the locals – for whatever part of the country you're interested in.

Virtual Wales

Perhaps you're thinking of moving from one area to another, and you want to know where the best schools are, or how much council tax you'll have to pay. No problem – there are plenty of people you can talk to in the Local Life chat rooms, which are Hosted each day by people from different cities or regions around the country. Just visit AOL Keyword: **LL Chat** to get started. There are separate areas for every part of Britain. You can even chat in Welsh at AOL Keyword: **Virtual Wales**.

And as well as the chat rooms, the Local Life channel has plenty of message boards, where you can post your queries about different parts of the country, so you can plan a great day out, or find people to meet in the pub the same day you move in.

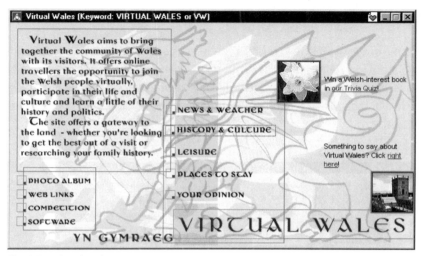

Fig. 8.7 Virtual Wales.

Love and relationships

Everyone wants a satisfying love life, and there are plenty of places on AOL where you can find help and advice, whether it's how to overcome your shyness and make the first approach to someone, or things to do on a first date.

| Love Chat |

| Personals |

Why not wander along to AOL Keyword: **Love Chat**, where you can talk or flirt with people in the chat rooms or message boards. But remember, these boards are for talking, not blind dates. If you're after that sort of excitement, why not make a posting in the AOL Keyword: **Personals** area, and see if anyone responds?

| Families |

| Gay |

Some of the hardest relationships you'll ever have to deal with are those with your children, or your parents. AOL provides plenty of space to let off steam or seek advice, at AOL Keyword: **Families**. And whatever your sexuality or race, you'll find people like you on AOL – just check out AOL Keyword: **Lifestyles Chat**.

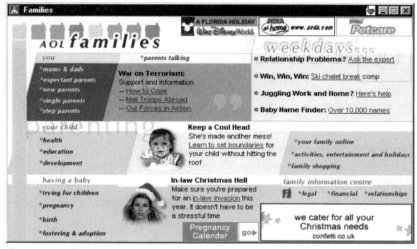

Fig. 8.8 Families.

News and sport

Sport Chat

If there's one thing that's guaranteed to be a good way of bringing people together, it's sport, and AOL has plenty of areas where sports fans can get together and talk about teams, players, and the latest match. You'll find it all at AOL Keyword: **Sport Chat**. Whatever the major sporting event of the day, you'll find a message board where you can chat about it, whether it's the likelihood of the UK teams losing, or the prospects for our brightest Olympic stars.

You'll find chat rooms for lots of the main sports, including football, rugby, horse racing, motorsport, and even WWF wrestling. Just click on the sport you're interested in, and you'll be able to chat with other fans, or wait for the Hosted chats every evening.

Fig. 8.9   Sport Chat.

News Chat

And current affairs are catered for too. As soon as any major news story breaks on AOL's Welcome screen, you'll find members gathering at AOL Keyword: **News Chat** to swap the latest information and talk about what it means for them. Why not join them, and hear the word on the street without leaving home?

Science

Scitech Messages

Scitech Chat

You'll find lots to talk about in the science area too, with message boards covering all sorts of topics, including science in the news. Visit AOL Keyword:

Scitech Messages and you'll find things like a message board to discuss Foot and Mouth Disease, and discussions about space, astronomy, and even UFOs. There's a science and technology chat room too, at AOL Keyword: **Scitech Chat**, so you can gossip about things as diverse as the space shuttle or GM crop trials.

And finally...

Those are more than 30 of the best AOL Keywords to visit for chatting, posting messages and seeking help, advice or inspiration from AOL. But that's only the beginning – there are many, many more places that you can visit online, whether you want to meet old friends, find the solution to a problem, or just pass the time of day.

Chat

If you like chat and think you have what it takes to help other people out with their problems, you can even volunteer to be an AOL Host – though you do need to have been a member for at least four months.

You can find out more simply by visiting AOL Keyword: **Chat**, or clicking **Chat and Communities** on the channel list, where there are also links to more message boards and chat rooms.

Next, though, we'll have a look at some of the ways you can keep in touch with your AOL friends and colleagues, even when you're away from your computer. AOL Anywhere means that, once you've met people online, it's easier than you ever imagined to keep in touch, no matter where you are in the world.

CHAPTER

9

AOL Anywhere

By now, you're probably a past master at using AOL to communicate with friends, family, colleagues, and plenty of other people too. But while AOL is installed on your own computer, aren't you tied to that when you want to chat?

AOL Anywhere

Well, the answer is actually No, thanks to what AOL call **AOL Anywhere**. That's the name for a range of things that make it possible for you to sign on to AOL from just about anywhere, whether you're using a computer, a PDA, or even a mobile phone on the move.

*If you're visiting a friend and they have AOL installed on their computer, you can access the service too – just pick Guest from the list of Screen Names, click **Sign On**, and you'll be asked to enter your own Screen Name and password.*

What it offers

AOL Anywhere doesn't give you access to all the features of AOL, like the chat rooms, or the special areas like online editions of magazines. But it does allow you to do one of the most important things – communicate.

Depending on how you connect, AOL Anywhere can give you access to your email, your Buddy List groups, Instant Message, and the Groups@AOL facility.

So as long as you can get to a computer with an Internet connection and a Web browser, you'll be able to check your emails, send Instant Messages, and look at the pages for any Groups that you're a member of.

If you have a computer with the AOL Instant Messenger™ software installed, you'll be able to join private chats with groups of your friends, and send them files or even chat live.

On a WAP mobile phone, you can access your Buddy List and send Instant Messages; you'll be able to read your emails, compose new ones and send them. If it's just a quick reply, you can even create a standard response on your PC and choose it from your mobile phone!

So, AOL Anywhere ensures you can always keep in touch – but it goes one better than that.

The AOL Instant Messenger service isn't just a way for you to catch up with Instant Messages when you're away from your AOL account. It's open to absolutely everyone on the Internet.

That means that you're not just restricted to sending Instant Messages to people on AOL. Colleagues and friends who use other Internet providers or access the Net at work can still be reached – all they have to do is download and install the AOL Instant Messenger™ software.

If you're not an AOL member, you have to register a Screen Name to use Instant Messenger, but it's completely free, so tell your friends to sign up. And when they have, they can use the same screen name to join any of the Groups you've created using the Groups@AOL facility.

AOL On Your Palm

AOL On Your Mobile

So, now you know what AOL Anywhere is all about, let's look at how to use it. We'll start by showing you how to access your email when you're away from your home computer. Later on you can find out how to access AOL from your electronic organiser with **AOL On Your Palm**, and how to use AOL with your mobile phone, via **AOL On Your Mobile**.

Don't forget that AOL Anywhere is always being added to or updated, to help you keep in touch and make the most of the latest ways of communicating. You can find out the latest on the AOL Anywhere mini-channel – just click **AOL Anywhere** on the channels toolbar in AOL, or go to AOL Keyword: **AOL Anywhere**.

AOL Mail

Have you ever wanted to send an email from your holiday, telling everyone in the office what a wonderful time you're having?

Or perhaps you're visiting a client, and you want to check to see if that important quotation has arrived via email.

You might be wanting to check your messages before you leave work, to make sure that tonight's dinner date is still on.

Whatever the situation, AOL Mail lets you access your messages from anywhere. You just need to find a computer with an Internet connection and a Web browser.

Enter the address http://www.aol.co.uk/ in the Web browser – usually you just type it in the bar at the top, just like entering an AOL Keyword or Web address when you're using AOL. When the AOL home page displays, you'll see a screen like this one appear.

Fig. 9.1   Signing on to AOL Mail.

All you have to do is type your AOL Screen Name and password, and click to sign in. You may be asked to click again on the next screen as part of AOL's security, to ensure that no one can read your mail as it's accessed over the Internet.

Although AOL mail is secure, if you're using a Web browser in a public place like a cybercafé, it's a good idea to quit the browser completely (usually an option on the **File** *menu) when you've finished. That will ensure that all the details of your mail are removed from the browser, for maximum security.*

After you're signed on to AOL Mail, you'll see a main screen which is very like the screens you see when you use AOL on your own computer – just click on a message to read it, or click on the tabs at the top of the screen to look at Old or Sent Mail. The **Write** button pops up a new window to create messages.

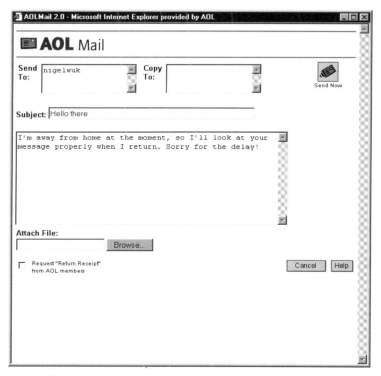

Fig. 9.2 Writing an email using AOL Mail.

There are a few differences, of course. When you're using AOL Mail you can't compose messages with different typefaces, and so on. You have to use ordinary text. And you won't have access to your address book – now's the time to memorise or write down those important email addresses.

When you read a message using AOL Mail, it's moved to the Old Mail area of your mailbox, so you'll have to look there to see it when you're back home using AOL on your computer. Select the message and click **Keep As New** *if you want the message to stay in your list of new mail to read when you get home.*

AIM

AIM stands for AOL Instant Messenger, and it's a program that you can install to give you access to Instant Message, and plenty of other features.

AIM is free, and you can always download the latest version from http://www.aol.co.uk/aim. Friends who aren't AOL members can download it and sign up for a Screen Name at the same time, so you'll be able to send them messages.

You'll also be able to see them in your Buddy List™, whether you're connected via the AOL software at home or using AIM in the office or even on a mobile.

Registering a screen name for AIM

If you're reading this section of the book and you don't have an AOL account, then the first thing you need to do is register a Screen Name; AOL members can skip to the next section, *Getting started with AIM*.

You might already have an AOL Screen Name! If you registered for Netscape's NetCenter or Netscape Messenger, you can use the same name and password for AIM.

A Screen Name is just a sort of nickname that's used to identify you to the AOL computers. Each Screen Name has to be unique – so if you try to pick one like John Smith, it's almost certainly been taken already. It doesn't cost anything at all to register a Screen Name, and it makes you part of one of the largest online communities in the world! Remember, if you want access to the whole of AOL, you'll still need to pay a monthly subscription – this Screen Name is just for free, public services provided by AOL.

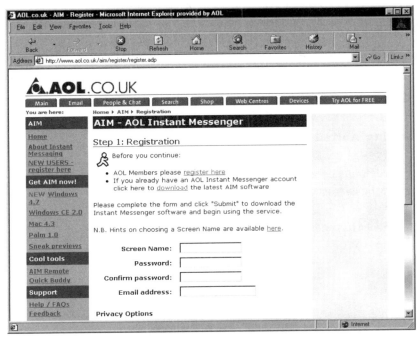

Fig. 9.3   Registering a Screen Name for AIM.

You'll be asked to sign up for a Screen Name as the first step in downloading AIM from the Web site. Just type the name that you'd like to use, along with a password and click the Submit button.

If the name you picked has already been taken, you'll be asked to try again. Once you've found a name that's available, you'll be registered, and a confirmation email will be sent to your email address. Don't forget to reply to it!

If you can't get your first choice of name, try adding something like your town or county to the end of it, like FredSmithUK, or JleeBucks.

The Screen Name that you register with AIM can be used for all the free public AOL services that you can access on the Internet, including Groups@AOL (see **Chapter 7, Groups and Web Sites**) and AIM Express (see **AIM Express** below). You won't be able to create AOL Groups if you're not a paid-up AOL member, but you'll be able to join in Groups that have been created by other members.

7 Groups@AOL

9 AIM Express

Getting started with AIM

If you've just downloaded AIM from the AOL Web site, you'll have a file on your computer called AIM Installer. All you need to do is double-click on it and follow the instructions to install the software.

When AIM has been installed, double-click on its icon and the Sign On screen appears.

Fig. 9.4   The AIM Sign On screen.

Just type in your Screen Name and password and press **Enter**.

AIM can remember your password, and even connect automatically each time you start it – just click to put a check mark in the two boxes on the Sign On screen. Remember that if you do save the password, anyone with access to your computer can sign on with your screen name.

When you press Enter, AIM will connect to AOL's computers and then you'll be led through a setup wizard, which can help you find people you might want to chat to, and register some of your interests, so that people can find and talk with you. When you've finished with the wizard – or if you click to skip it – the Buddy List window will appear.

Fig. 9.5 The AIM Buddy List window.

Of course, to start with, there won't be any buddies in the list – AIM doesn't know who you saved as buddies in the AOL software on your computer.

Adding your friends is very easy, though. At the top of the Buddy List window you'll see two tabs – **Online** and **Setup**. Just click the **Setup** tab, and then click with the mouse on the group that you'd like to add a buddy to.

At the bottom of the list, you'll see a few buttons; click the **Add Buddy** icon, which is a single person with a + sign next to them. An entry will appear in your Buddy List window, called New User.

All you have to do now is edit the text to change it from New User to the name of the buddy that you want to add.

You can split your Buddy List into groups, for example colleagues, club members, family, and so on, by clicking the **Add Group** *icon, which shows a group of people with a + sign. Change the name from New Group to whatever you like, and either add buddies to the group, or drag existing ones onto the group name to move them.*

After adding buddies to your list, click the **Online** tab again, and you'll see their names in grey if they're not connected, or black if they are.

Sending and receiving Instant Messages

All you have to do to send an Instant Message is double-click on a buddy's name, type the message in the box that appears, and click **Send**.

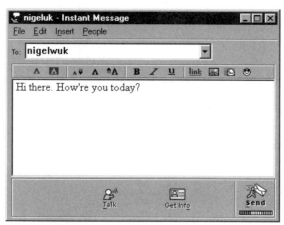

Fig. 9.6   Sending an Instant Message with AIM.

As you can see, there are a few other buttons on the Instant Message box. You can use them to add smileys, for example, or to send messages with a different colour and typeface. You can even add a Web link to your message – so you could invite a friend to visit and send them a link to a Web site that shows where your home is.

AIM really is just as simple to use as sending Instant Messages using the AOL software – but now you'll be able to keep in touch with buddies wherever you are, as long as there's a computer you can install AIM on.

When you receive an Instant Message it will pop up on your screen looking something like this; just type your response in the bottom box, and click **Send**.

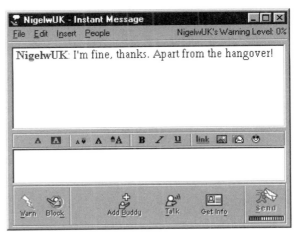

Fig. 9.7   Receiving a message with AIM.

Chatting with your buddies

AIM isn't just about swapping messages between two people. You can use it to make your own private chat room too. It's a little like using an AOL chat room – you could arrange to be online with your buddies at a particular time, for example, and talk about the trip you're planning to a theme park.

You could even use a Buddy Chat as an alternative to getting everyone at work into a meeting room. Why waste time wandering around the building when you can invite all the relevant people to join you in a chat room, and explain your latest idea?

To create a chat room, click on the names you want to chat with in your Buddy List window, and then click **Chat**. AIM will suggest a name for the chat room, which you can change if you want.

Fig. 9.8   Inviting buddies for a chat with AIM.

You can even give people a reason for the chat, like 'Marketing meeting for new season.' Click **Send** to invite everyone, and they'll all receive a message on screen inviting them to the chat room. All they need to do is click **Go Chat**, and they'll join you there.

The chat room looks very similar to an AOL chat room, with a list of the participants on the right, the discussion in the main window, and an area at the bottom where you can type your own comments. Press **Enter** or click **Send**, and your words will appear in the chat room for everyone else to see. You can even include a link to an Internet site, if you like, using **Link**.

Fig. 9.9 An AIM chat room.

Buddy Chat rooms are only accessible to people using AIM. If you want to chat with an AOL member, they'll need to run AIM too, which they can do while they're still connected to AOL.

Advanced AIM

Actually, AIM can do a lot more than just send Instant Messages or create chat rooms. You can swap files, include pictures in your messages, and even talk with other people!

Not all the AIM features are available in every version, but you can find out what someone can do by moving the mouse pointer over their name when they're connected. The box that appears will tell you which of the AIM features they have available to them.

We could actually dedicate a whole book just to using AIM and its more advanced features, but we'll give you an idea of them here.

If you're an AOL subscriber, you might wonder why you should install AIM on your computer. The advanced features, like swapping pictures, are one good reason, and if you download the latest version of AIM – that's 4.7 or later – you can run it at the same time as AOL, to receive Instant Messages and access all the advanced features of AIM too.

All you have to do to make sure your Instant Messages appear in AIM instead of AOL is select one of the Away Messages at the bottom of your AOL Buddy List window, and then chat to people using AIM instead. Then you can enjoy all the features of both AOL and AIM at the same time!

Sending pictures via AIM

Have you ever wondered what the person you're chatting with looks like? If you're signed on to AOL, you can of course send someone a picture via email. But AIM can go one better than that.

You can put a picture right in the middle of a message. On the **People** menu, just choose **Open IM image connection**. The person you're chatting with will see a warning on their screen, and they have to click to confirm that they want to receive an image from you – so you don't need to worry that people will send you unsolicited pictures when you use AIM.

Once the connection is made, you can click the picture icon in the Instant Message window, and you'll be asked to choose the picture that you want to send.

Unlike sending an ordinary Instant Message, your picture won't be passed through AOL's computers. Instead it's sent directly from your computer to your buddy's – so the time it takes will depend on how fast their connection to the Internet is.

Try to keep pictures small, and save them in the JPEG format, so that you can send them quickly via AIM.

If you don't want to wait while pictures are sent via email, using Instant Message is a great way to send them. Imagine if you're taking photographs – you could transfer them from a digital camera to a computer in a couple of moments and then send them via AIM to a friend or family member.

Sending files via AIM

It's not just pictures that you can send, either. You can send any type of file that's on your computer, so you could transfer a bit of work you're been doing at home to a colleague in their office. Or perhaps your printer is out of ink, and you want a friend to print out the party invitations you've designed.

With AIM, you can send them the file, and point out anything you need to, or answer any questions they have, far more easily than sending emails to and fro.

To send a file is easy. All you need to do is click on a buddy's name in the Buddy List window, and choose **Send File**, or click **Send File** on the **People** menu at the top of the Instant Message window, if you're already having a conversation with them.

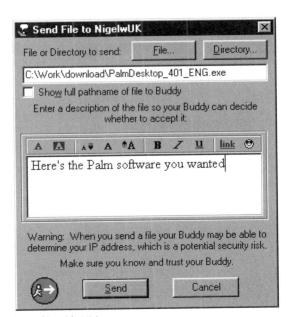

Fig. 9.10 Sending a file with AIM.

When this screen appears, just choose the file that you want to send, and add a brief description of it, then click **Send**.

> *Try to make the description useful, so that people know whether or not they should accept it; if a stranger is sending you a file, or you're not sure what's being sent to you, then the safest thing to do is to reject it.*

Share and share alike

Even better, with AIM you don't have to be talking to people to swap files with them.

Instead, you can share a folder on your computer, and people can fetch files from it when they want to.

You could share the pictures of your new baby, for example, or some files at work, just in case you need them when you're at home over the weekend.

To set up file sharing, you need to choose the Preferences option from the AIM menus: click **My AIM**, choose **Edit Options**, then **Edit Preferences**, and when the preferences screen appears, click **File Sharing**, then **File Transfer**.

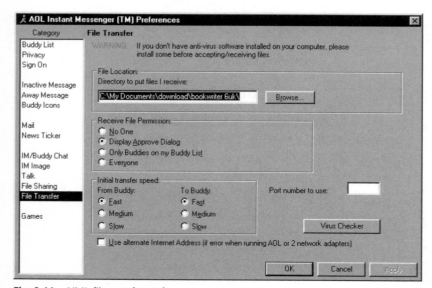

Fig. 9.11 AIM's file transfer preferences.

You can choose the folders that you want to share with other users from these screens, and choose whether everyone can access your files, only people listed on your Buddy List, or even just people in a particular group of your Buddy List – so you could, for instance, just allow family members to access pictures from your computer.

When someone wants to look at one of the files you're sharing, or if you want to get a file from someone else, just choose their name, right-click, and select **Get File** from the menu to see a list of what's available.

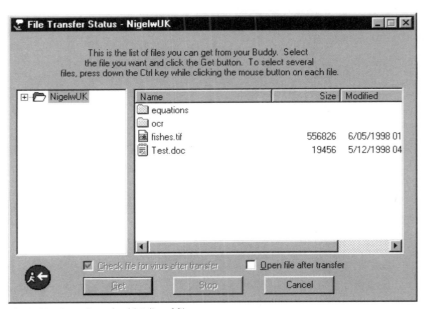

Fig. 9.12   Browsing a buddy's list of files.

Before you share files with other people via AOL Instant Messenger, you should make sure you have anti-virus software installed on your computer; files are not checked by AOL. If you don't know what a file is, or you don't trust the source, don't allow it onto your computer.

AIM voice

As well as sending pictures and files, you can even use AIM as a kind of Internet telephone system. As the bottom of the window when you're sending an Instant Message to someone, you'll see a button labelled **Talk**. It also appears in Buddy Chat rooms, when you highlight a member in the list of people present.

When you click **Talk**, your computer will attempt to connect directly to your buddy's and they'll be asked if they want to accept the connection.

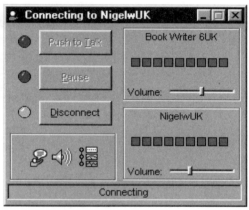

Fig. 9.13   Talking via AIM and your sound card.

The Talk screen shows the sound level, so you can alter the volume if your buddy sounds faint, or send louder sounds to them. The options available will depend on the type of sound card that you have in your computer. For example, you may not be able to talk while you're listening to your buddy speak. Use **Push To Talk** when you want to speak, just like a two-way radio, and click **Disconnect** when you're done.

The quality may not be as good as when you're chatting on the phone, but it's a great way to keep in touch with people around the world. All you'll pay is the cost of connecting to AOL – which is at most a local call, and if you're on an AOL Flat Rate plan, it's nothing at all.

Voice connections aren't available in all versions of AIM; move the mouse pointer over a buddy's name in your list to see if they can talk with you.

AIM safety and privacy

AIM has its own security system, so you'll need to set it up separately if you want to block messages from certain people, or only allow them from some. Select the Preferences in AIM, via the **My AIM** menu, and click **Privacy**.

On this screen, you can choose whether to restrict communications to people on your Buddy List, or to allow everyone to speak with you. You can also create a new list of people on this screen, which can be used to specify either people to allow to talk with you, or people to refuse.

Although AIM has privacy settings, they can always be changed. The best way to keep your children safe online is to supervise their use of the computer.

When you're using AIM, you'll also notice a box at the bottom of the messages that people send you, labelled **Warn**, together with a little graph showing a warning level.

The warning system allows you to inform the AOL computers if you think someone is behaving inappropriately – for example if they're asking you for password information, or harassing you.

When the warning level of a user is increased to a certain level, AIM will restrict what they are able to do – it's like a built-in policeman, to stop anyone from upsetting other users.

Next to the **Warn** button is one labelled **Block**; if you click on it, then the person who's just sent you a message will be blocked from sending any more to you.

Other useful AIM features

AIM has plenty of other useful features, but we'll just mention a couple more here. Click **My AIM** and choose **Away Message**, for example, and you can either choose a pre-written message, or type in a new one.

Fig. 9.14 Creating an Away Message.

What's the point of this? Well, if you're working, for example, you might want to leave AIM running so you can see if your partner signs on, but you don't really want to be disturbed too much.

When you've set an Away Message, anyone who sends you an Instant Message will receive it automatically, so if you're too busy to respond, they won't think you're being rude – unless you typed a rude Away Message, of course!

Another handy feature is profiles; you can create a Profile for AIM which will be stored on AOL's computers, giving people a little more information about yourself – it could be the place where you live, or what you look like, or your favourite foods – whatever you want to say.

You can update your Profile from the **My AIM** menu, and you can also search for other people that way too, if you want to find new friends to talk with.

AIM on the go – AIM Express

By now, you should have realised quite how useful AIM can be. But of course, you need to download it onto your computer.

What happens if you're on holiday, and you can only access the Net via a cybercafé? Or perhaps you promised your partner you'd check in with a quick message at 7pm, but you're still in a client's office, and you can't really install extra software on their computer.

Don't worry – there's a solution just for you. Called AIM Express, it's a cut-down version of AIM that runs in your Web browser. All you need is a connection to the Internet and a Web browser that understands Java.

You can access AIM Express by going to the Web address http://www.aol.co.uk/ aim and following the links to AIM Express or Quick Buddy (the old name for AIM Express). Click **Start**, and after a short pause, the AIM Express window will appear, with boxes for you to type in your Screen Name and password. Click **Sign-on** and you'll be connected to AIM.

As you can see in Fig. 9.15, AIM Express looks very similar to the full version of AIM, though you can only send Instant Messages or join Buddy Chats with it. To add a new buddy, click **Add** at the top of the screen, or choose the **Edit** option to edit the Buddy List and the Block/Allow list.

Once you're used to AIM, you'll find Express very simple, and if you do get stuck, then help is always just a click away.

Palm Mail

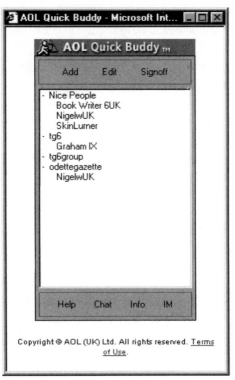

Fig. 9.15 AIM Express

AOL On Your Palm

All the things we've looked at so far may be really handy, but they rely on you being able to reach a computer connected to the Internet. And while computers are fairly common, you won't always be able to find a cybercafé, or someone who'll let you sit at their desk to check your mail.

No matter – another part of AOL Anywhere is giving you access to AOL when you're not at a computer, and AOL for Palm is one of the most important parts of that. You can find it online at AOL Keyword: **Palm Mail**.

AOL Mail for Palm is a cut-down AOL program that runs on Palm OS devices, like the Palm V or Handspring Visor. All you need to do is install the AOL software on your Palm device, and then tell it to connect to the AOL network.

If you are using a mobile phone to connect to AOL, remember that a number that may be free to call when you access AOL at home may not be free when called from a mobile. You should check with your mobile phone operator if you are not sure how much calls will cost. AOL's fixed rate call options do not apply to calls made from mobile phones, and you may incur additional fees.

With AOL Mail On Your Palm, you can compose, read and send emails, check your Buddy List window to see who's online, and exchange Instant Messages with other AOL and AIM users.

Fig. 9.16 The main screen of AOL On Your Palm.

If you're used to AOL on your PC or Macintosh, you should find AOL On Your Palm pretty easy to get to grips with. The main screen lets you choose your online mailbox, read new messages, or look at messages in a filing cabinet stored on your Palm. You can use the filing cabinet to keep track of messages that you've read, or to edit ones that you've written already.

AOL On Your Palm even has an AutoAOL option, so you can tell it to sign on and collect all your messages so that you can read them at your leisure and compose replies to send the next time you connect.

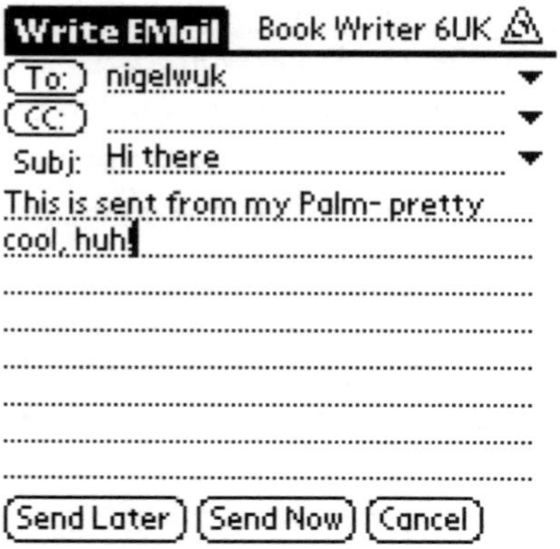

Fig. 9.17 Writing an email on your Palm PDA.

As you can see, the Write Email screen is very simple. Best of all, it links directly to the address book on your Palm, so you can tap on **To** or **Cc** and just select the email address that you want to send from all the contacts you have stored!

Just write your message, and tap **Send Later** to put the message in your Waiting mail list, or **Send Now** if you're connected to AOL.

Fig. 9.18 The Buddy List screen in AOL for Palm.

Unlike a desktop computer, on a Palm there's not much space to show all the Instant Messages that might pop up, so when you view your Buddy List window, you'll see a special icon next to any buddies that you're having a conversation with.

You can tap on a name to select that buddy and send a message to them, or to go to a conversation you're already having via Instant Message – and when a new message arrives, you'll hear a beep, and the icon in the top right of the Palm screen will flash, too.

And to save you having to update your Buddy List window, AOL for Palm automatically retrieves the Buddy List groups that you created with your AOL account – and any changes you make when you're using the Palm version will be reflected the next time you sign on from your computer.

AOL On Your Mobile

You can still keep in touch with AOL when you're out and about, as long as you have a WAP mobile phone. With AOL On Your Mobile, you can access your AOL account, check your email on the move and send Instant Messages to your buddies, as well as looking up information such as film listings for your local cinema, or the latest news.

AOL On Your Mobile

You can find out more about AOL Mobile at AOL Keyword: **AOL On Your Mobile**, where you also have to sign up to use the service. Once you have signed up, you will be given a personal URL, which you can bookmark on your phone to provide easy access to AOL On Your Mobile without having to tap in your Screen Name and password.

Remember, although AOL On Your Mobile is a free service, your mobile phone company may charge you for the phone call to access AOL On Your Mobile. These costs aren't included in your AOL subscription.

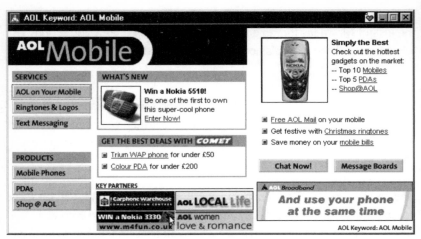

Fig. 9.19 The AOL Mobile main screen.

*After you've signed up for AOL On Your Mobile, the service can be customised for your needs. At AOL Keyword: **AOL On Your Mobile** you will see an option to 'Customise the service'. Here you can add people to your mobile address book to make sending emails from your phone simple. You can also choose what type of news you access on your phone, what cinema you get listings for and even the default star sign of the daily on-phone horoscope.*

Reading your mail with AOL On Your Mobile

Once you've customised the service, it's time to try connecting to AOL from your phone. On most phones, if you try to access the personal URL that you have bookmarked on your mobile phone, the phone will automatically dial your mobile phone provider's number to connect you to the Internet (remember this call may not be free). If it doesn't, consult your phone's documentation or contact your mobile phone provider to check that your phone is enabled for WAP. The email option is the first item on the list after you've signed on. If you have new messages, you'll be told right away.

The first three options correspond to the three sections of your AOL mailbox, and the last lets you write a new message on your phone. When you read an email message on your phone, you'll have the normal email options available to you – reply, reply to all, forward, keep as new and delete. All do exactly the same as when you're using AOL on your own computer. However, due to the limitations of mobile phone memory, it is impossible to save the email to your Personal Filing Cabinet or download any attachments.

Fig. 9.20   The email display on a mobile phone.

When you choose **Email**, you'll see a display a little like this one.

Writing a message with AOL On Your Mobile

When you write an email on your mobile phone, the first thing you do is enter the email addresses of the recipients. You can either tap in the email addresses here or you can select them from your address book if you have entered your friends into your AOL On Your Mobile address book at AOL Keyword: **AOL On Your Mobile** when you customised the service.

Once you've done that, you need to click the option **Enter Subject and Body**, which will take you to the next screen. Here you fill in the text of your email and then choose **Send**.

AOL On Your Mobile can, of course, be used for plenty of other things besides sending and receiving email, but since this book is just about communicating,

Fig. 9.21   Addressing a message in AOL Mobile.

that's all we've had space for. If you want to find out more, just visit AOL Key-word: **AOL On Your Mobile** when you're using your PC, and you can find out what other things it will do.

CHAPTER

10

Online Guidelines

We've all heard that there are some people online that, frankly, you'd prefer not to meet – and you certainly wouldn't want your children to meet. But don't worry! The good news is that the vast majority of people you'll meet online are just like yourself – honest, ordinary people who will help out if they can.

To help make sure that you don't run into any problems, AOL provides special Parental Controls that will help you restrict who can contact your children and Mail Controls so you can stop anyone who might be annoying you from sending you email. There are also people on hand to help if you need any assistance and reporting mechanisms in place.

And just like any society or group of people, there are rules, regulations, and guidelines for the way you should act, often called netiquette.

That's what this chapter is all about – how to make sure you stay safe online, and don't do anything that will upset or inconvenience other users. In short, if you follow the guidelines here, you'll know what to do, and where to turn to for help if you're confused.

Help is at hand

Whatever you're doing on AOL, help and assistance are just a couple of clicks away. Two of the most important things you can call on are the AOL Guides and Hosts, who are real people who are there to help out with any problems.

Hosts are found in specific areas of AOL, while Guides roam more freely across all the areas, and you'll be able to spot them in chat rooms easily, since no one else can have the words Guide or Host in their screen name.

You can talk with a Guide or a Host by posting on a message board, or chatting with them in a chat room. They'll be able to answer questions about how to use the AOL software, where to find the information you're looking for, or even tell other users off for behaving inappropriately.

Trouble

If there's no Guide or Host around when you need one, all you have to do is go to AOL Keyword: **Trouble** and you'll see a screen like this one.

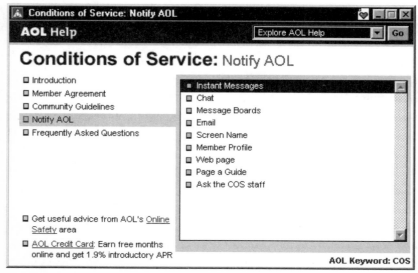

Fig. 10.1 Use the Trouble screen to summon help.

Guide Pager

Trouble

Rules

You can report Conditions of Service violations directly to AOL's COS team by choosing the most appropriate button, depending on where the violation took place (eg. Instant Message, Chat or message boards). If there is a serious problem in a chat room, use AOL Keyword: **Guide Pager** *to summon a guide, but be sure to report the problem first at AOL Keyword:* **Trouble**. *The Conditions of Service can be found at AOL Keyword:* **Rules**.

AAA

If it's problems using AOL that are bugging you, there's a separate place to visit. Go to AOL Keyword: **AAA** – it stands for All About AOL – and you'll see a screen giving you easy access to common questions and answers, a glossary, and a quick tour of AOL. It's especially useful for new users, who will find most problems solved in the Frequently Asked Questions area.

Tech

The AOL Keyword: **Tech Chat** area is another good place to go if you're having difficulties using any part of the AOL service. You'll be able to talk directly with one of the support team, who can help you through whatever you're trying to do – it's often easier to do that than to try and explain things over the phone.

Of course, if you do get stuck, AOL's helpline is available to members until midnight every day, and calls are completely free. All you need to do is dial 0800 376 5432 (or 1800 60 50 40 in the Republic of Ireland).

As well as Guides and Hosts, another important thing that AOL provides to help keep you safe and secure online is Parental Controls.

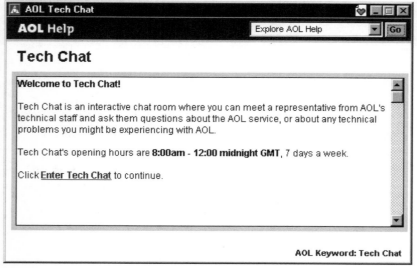

Fig. 10.2 The Technical Support screen.

Parental Controls allow you to help restrict what certain members of your family can do when they use your AOL account – you can create up to six additional names on your account, with a different password and set of privileges for each one.

Later on in this chapter, we'll explain how you can use the Parental Controls to choose what sort of communication each member of your family can access. First, though, let's look at a few of the basic rules that should help to ensure that you fit quickly and easily into the online community.

Face to face

When you're communicating with people online, one of the things that's missing is body language, and that can make it hard to tell whether someone's smiling or frowning.

To make it easier to interpret what people mean, over the years a sort of shorthand has evolved amongst people online, using a combination of abbreviations and smileys or 'emoticons.'

Anyone who uses mobile phone text messages might be familiar with some of these already, but to help you along, here are some of the most common.

If the smileys don't seem to make much sense, try turning your head on its side and then looking at them – they're supposed to look a little like a face. We've just included some of the most common ones here – there are plenty of others around, though they're not used so much. If you're not sure what someone means, don't be afraid to ask, or look at AOL Keyword: **Smileys**, where you can find a more complete listing.

> Smileys

Smileys
:-) Smiling, happy

:-(Unhappy

:-| Straight faced

;-) Winking

>:-) Surprised

Abbreviations
AAMOF As a matter of fact

AFAICT As far as I can tell (or Remember)

BTW By the way

CU See you

IMHO In my humble opinion

ROFL Rolls on floor laughing

RTFM Read the flaming manual

TTBOMK To the best of my knowledge

Common sense

AOL has set of rules called the Conditions of Service that form part of the contract between you and them; you can read them at AOL Keyword: **COS**.

Of course, it's not just other AOL members that you can communicate with – there are millions of people on the Internet too, and they're not necessarily bound to agree to the same sort of conditions.

Nevertheless, there is a set of conventions, called netiquette, that's grown up over the years. They're mostly based on common sense, and as long as you follow them, you should get along just fine with everyone that you meet online.

- Always think before you click **Send**; it's easy to respond quickly without thinking – and that means you can upset someone in an instant.

- Don't type something that you wouldn't say face to face.

- Remember that it's not always obvious when you type something that you mean it as a joke. You can put a smiley after your words, but telling someone they're a fat cow might still upset them even if you do!

- DON'T TYPE ALL IN CAPITAL LETTERS. It's not as easy to read as ordinary mixed letters, and is the online equivalent of shouting.

- Don't send people files without asking them if it's OK first. Some people have to pay to receive their messages, and a large file means they'll have to stay online longer.

- Don't pass on chain letters. No matter how important they seem to be, or how reputable the sources, it's bad form to pass these on. Get rich quick schemes annoy people, and virus warnings that arrive via email are almost always hoaxes.

- In message boards or other discussion areas, it's usually a good idea to sit and watch for a while before joining in. You might see your question answered without having to ask, and you'll get a feel for how the community works.

- Always check to see if there is a FAQ – a list of Frequently Asked Questions – that gives you the information you're looking for. That way, you'll save people from having to answer the same things over and over again.

As you can see, there's nothing complicated or mysterious in netiquette – it's all about making sure everyone gets on as smoothly as possible and using your common sense.

It's a good idea to use AOL yourself for a while and get the feeling of how to do things online before you create additional names for other people in your family. That way you'll be able to answer questions about netiquette for them – and remember that as the holder of an AOL account, you're ultimately responsible for what people who use your account do when they're online.

It's all in the name

When you signed up for AOL, you created a Screen Name to use for yourself, which is called a Master Screen Name. You can use your Master Screen Name to create additional names on your AOL account for other members of the family, or if you just want a different name for work and play.

Each name that you create can be used to send and receive email, chat via Instant Message, and do all the other things that you do with your Master Screen Name, except create more names.

What's more important is that you can assign different levels of privilege to all the names on your account using the AOL Keyword: **Parental Controls** screen, and only you will be able to change the settings by refining your choice.

To get started with creating a new Screen Name, all you have to do is visit AOL Keyword: **Screen Names**, and you'll see a screen like this one.

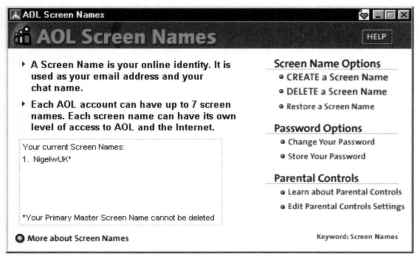

Fig. 10.3   Creating extra Screen Names for your account.

Just follow the instructions on the screen, and you can set up a new name in hardly any time at all – with a total of seven names available on your AOL account. As the last stage in creating a new Screen Name, you can choose a Parental Controls category to suit the age of the person who'll be using the name. Just pick the most appropriate option – you can change the settings easily, as we'll explain in a moment.

Remember there's no extra fee for the names you add, but only one of them can be connected to AOL at the same time.

That means, for example, that if you install AOL on your office and home computers, you can't use it in both places at the same time, even with different Screen Names.

Even though you can't sign on with the AOL software in two places at once, you can use your Screen Names for other AOL services accessed via the Internet, like the AOL Instant Messenger™ service. So, you could let your children use the computer at home to connect to AOL with their Screen Name and you can sign on to AIM in the office with your own name, and send messages to and fro. See **Chapter 9, AOL Anywhere** *for further details.*

9 AIM

Parental Controls

Safety first

The rules of netiquette that we've already looked at are all sensible and straightforward, and they're applicable to everyone who goes online. But there are some other points that you should bear in mind when you let your children go online. Explain these to them, to make sure that when they do talk with people, they have safety in mind..

- Children should only ever give their first name online. They shouldn't tell anyone online their full name, age, address, telephone number or where they go to school, or any other personal information that could identify them

- When you create a Member Profile for a child, never give any information that could identify them or where they live.

- Tell your children to ignore Instant Messages or emails from strangers. If they don't know who's sending them a message, they shouldn't reply.

- Try to keep an eye on what your children are doing when they use AOL and the Internet. Parental supervision is still the best way to keep kids safe!

- Make sure that they can talk to you about anything that could have upset them online just like they would do in the offline world.

Keeping in control

As well as the safety rules for kids, you can also set up other Screen Names for the rest of the family, which will allow you to use AOL's powerful Parental Controls feature to help decide what your children can access online.

For example, if you've given a young child access to AOL, wouldn't it be a good idea if you could make sure that they can only exchange email with a few people, like their grandparents and some other selected friends?

You might also want to be sure that they can't visit any of the areas of AOL or the Internet that, while OK for adults, might be a little unwelcoming to children – the news headlines discussion, for example.

Or maybe you'd like to give a teenage child a little more freedom to explore things on AOL and the rest of the Net, but without going into chat rooms.

Perhaps there's a particular person that you want to avoid – like a boss, or a former colleague that you've fallen out with, and you'd prefer it if they can't send emails to you.

Parental Controls can do all of this, very easily. Just go to AOL Keyword: **Parental Controls**, click **Set Parental Controls** and you'll see a screen like this one:

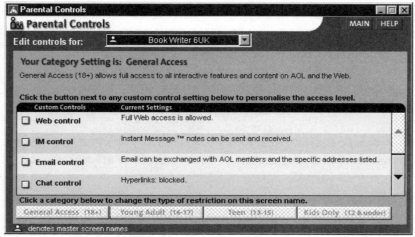

Fig. 10.4 Choosing Parental Controls settings.

The simplest way to use the Parental Controls is to select, for each Screen Name, one of the predefined categories that AOL has created.

All you need to do is select the Screen Name that you want to change from the list at the top of the screen, and then pick one of the categories: Kids Only, Young Teen, Mature Teen, or General Access.

Each of the categories automatically sets all the various options for the Screen Name you've chosen. For example, the Kids Only setting means that the Screen Name will only be able to access screens in the Kids channel of AOL and certain specially selected child-friendly Web sites. They can also only chat to people in the children's chat rooms, where there's always a Host or Guide present to give advice and information.

When you choose one of the categories, you'll see a brief description of what's allowed and what's not, but it doesn't stop there!

Customising the settings

But what about our example above, listing the people that one of your children can exchange messages with?

It's easy. As well as selecting one of the categories, you can scroll through the list of AOL features, and individually alter the different options. AOL will still remember the category that you put each Screen Name into, even if you change the options within that category.

Restricting Instant Messages

Let's begin by selecting who your child can receive Instant Messages from. Click **IM Control**, and you'll see a screen like this one.

You can block Instant Messages for this Screen Name, and the user won't be able to send or receive any Instant Messages at all.

Remember that even if you use Parental Controls to restrict Instant Messages when your child is signed on to AOL, those controls won't have

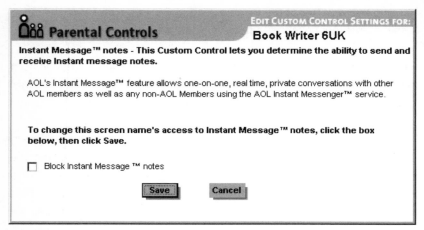

Fig. 10.5 Setting the Instant Message controls.

any effect if they sign on using the AOL Instant Messenger service, for example from a cybercafé on holiday. AIM has its own set of privacy settings, which you need to configure in the program itself. For maximum security, you should make sure that your child always uses the AOL software to chat with people, rather than AIM or similar programs.

Restricting email

Controlling who you can receive mail from is a little more complicated than setting up Instant Message. Click **Email control**, and you'll see a screen like this one.

As you can see, there's a list on the right, which will be empty to start with, and a box above where you can enter an email address or a domain, then click to add it to the list.

Down the left of the screen, the settings let you allow all mail, allow it from only other people on AOL, block it, or allow or block mail depending on the list of addresses and domains.

OK, you're probably wondering what a domain is. When you look at an email address, the domain is the part of it to the right of the @ symbol. So for an

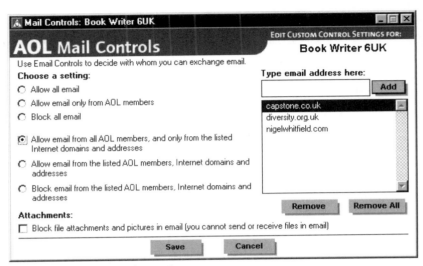

Fig. 10.6   Setting the email controls.

AOL user, the domain is aol.com. The Prime Minister's domain is number-10.gov.uk.

If you enter a domain in the list, you can block emails – or allow them – from anyone in that domain. For example, if your kids go to localschool.sch.uk, then adding that domain and allowing email from the listed address would mean all the people at that school could send them email.

If you just entered .gov.uk and said you wanted to block email from listed addresses and domains, then as well as blocking tony@number-10.gov.uk you'd also block mail from gordon@treasury.gov.uk, because they both end in .gov.uk

As you can see the email controls are very flexible – just set the options you want, and you can be sure you'll only receive messages from people you want.

You can only block or allow messages from people in the list – you can't block some, and allow others. So bear this in mind when you create your list, or it could have unexpected results.

Mail Controls

Spam

If you want to change your own email settings quickly, you can reach this screen at AOL Keyword: **Mail Controls***, rather than going through the Parental Controls screens. Mail Controls can only be set by your Master Screen Name, so don't worry about your kids changing what you've set!*

Remember that your Screen Name is your email address; if you create a Profile or visit an AOL chat room, people can see your name, and you may receive junk email as a result. At AOL Keyword: **Spam** *you can read tips on how to block some of the junk mail that you may receive. As we suggested in* **Chapter 2, Family and Friends***, you should consider creating a Screen Name just for chatting, with email to that name blocked, and don't create a Profile for your Master Screen Name.*

2 Profiles

Restricting chat rooms

Controlling access to chat rooms is easy too, but if you've selected Kids Only for the Screen Name, they'll only be able to access Kids Only chat anyway. Use this screen to stop your children chatting completely, if you prefer.

As you can see, there are quite a few options, but they're all self-explanatory. If you choose the first two options, then your children or family members will still be able to access the chat rooms on AOL's channels, but they'll be kept away from member-created rooms. You can use the last option to block links in chat rooms, so that even if someone does give out an inappropriate Web address, it can't be clicked on to view it.

Other controls

You'll find other controls in the Parental Controls section too, allowing you to restrict access to Web pages or other Internet areas, and you can even allow someone else to be a Master Screen Name on your account. If you do that

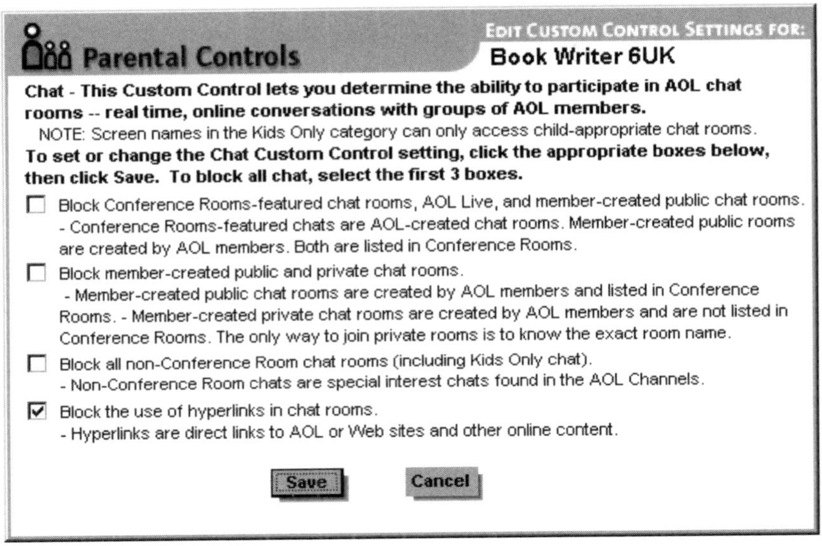

Fig. 10.7 Setting the Chat controls.

your spouse, for example, could create or delete other Screen Names if they wanted to.

Remember that if you make someone else a Master Screen Name, then they can change most of your AOL options too, or give more access to one of your children. You should always make sure the passwords for all your Master Screen Names are safe and secure.

Now you should know the basics of online safety, netiquette, and how to give other family members access to your AOL account. So sit back, relax, and enjoy communicating with AOL!

Index